TIME TO GET SERIOUS

FINDING

YOUR

MOMENT

OF

CLARITY

MICHAEL BART MATHEWS

TIME TO GET SERIOUS

FINDING
—YOUR—
MOMENT
—OF—
CLARITY

DISCOVER YOUR POWER WITHIN

MICHAEL BART MATHEWS

Order this book online at www.trafford.com
or email orders@trafford.com
Or www.tmeginc.com
email: info@tmeginc.com

Most Trafford titles are also available at major online book retailers.

Editor-In-Chief and Contributor: Robbie Mathews, President,
The Mathews Entrepreneur Group, Inc.

Print information available on the last page.

ISBN: 978-1-4907-9383-2 (sc)
ISBN: 978-1-4907-9382-5 (e)

Library of Congress Control Number: 2019934595

Because of the dynamic nature of the Internet, any web addresses or links contained in
this book may have changed since publication and may no longer be valid. The views
expressed in this work are solely those of the author and do not necessarily reflect the
views of the publisher, and the publisher hereby disclaims any responsibility for them.

Information provided in this book is for informational purposes only. This
information is NOT intended as a substitute or replacement for the advice
provided by your attorney, financial advisor, healthcare provider or any other
physician, or professional of your choice. Neither the lead author, co-authors, or
publisher shall be liable or responsible for any loss or damage allegedly arising
from any information, or suggestions of any kind from within this book.

Trafford rev. 03/12/2019

 www.trafford.com
North America & international
toll-free: 1 888 232 4444 (USA & Canada)
fax: 812 355 4082

CONTENTS

FINDING YOUR MOMENT OF CLARITY
YOUR JOURNEY TO SELF-IMPROVEMENT

MY GRATITUDE

Natalie Bonomo – United States
Peter Diaz – Australia
Adaku Ezeudo – Ireland
Elyse Falzone – United States
Emi Golding – Australia
Marja Katajisto – Finland/Switzerland
Robbie Mathews – United States
Amy Samaya – United States
Karel Vermeulen – South Africa

T his began as a local dream; however, it has expanded into a global vision! Your collaborative contributions to the completion of this creative process are all priceless! In the spirit of "let's help make this world a better place." together we are using, sharing and helping readers from around the world add more value to their everyday bravest journeys, called life. Our collective intent is to selflessly serve others.

Because of your unique Universal energy, light, awareness and high-frequency levels that govern how each one of us thinks, feel and act, I acknowledge my unwavering attitude of gratitude for your service rendered. Each one of you took time out of your own busy schedules, away from your family, and business to ensure the completion of this creative process.

I'm proud to say that there is no letter "I" in the word "TEAM" and together we made a great team. I am forever humble and grateful for this challenge and experience. Your individual credit of co-authorship of your intellectual property is represented in your own chapters and is duly noted.

I can't begin to thank you enough!

GRATITUDE FOR OUR READERS:

Thank you for purchasing this book. To gain access to your free bonus gift from Michael Bart Mathews, stop reading NOW! Go to www.tmeginc.com to claim your free bonus gift NOW; while they last! After you claim your gift, come back and continue on your journey to *"Finding Your Moment of Clarity."*

-Michael Bart Mathews

FOREWORD

By Adaku Ezeudo

I f you are ready to create a wonderful future for yourself and make quantum leaps in life, you have the right road map in your hands. What you have before you will teach you about investing in yourself so that you can manage yourself effectively regardless of what life might bring your way. This book will teach you how by simply changing the way you think, you can inevitably change your life. By making a commitment to improve yourself, build positive thought patterns and shed undesirable habits, you will begin a path to unlock your talents and abilities and experience new-found freedom you never thought was possible.

First, I must say it's a privilege to contribute to a relevant, timely and impactful piece of work by Michael "Bart" Mathews. I have studied his brilliant work over time and his sincere passion to positively impact the world one person at a time. He continues to share his wealth of wisdom and personal experience to inspire, educate and empower many to have better, happier and more fulfilled lives. He has sold many books aimed at inspiring others to be the best versions of themselves. Michael is one of the finest thinkers and writers on personal development and self-actualization. He has achieved outstanding results, for himself and many other people. His thinking in this book will inspire you to do the same for yourself and much more.

"Finding Your Moment of Clarity" shows you how to discover your innate resources and tap into your unique potentials. This book will get you to know who you truly are, your values, beliefs and the purpose you wish to pursue. It is a turning point in your life. While *"Finding Your Moment of*

Clarity." you will see what is really important in life. You are able to discover the habits that serve you and those that retard your personal growth. You will also learn to weed out any limiting way of thinking and replace them with empowering beliefs.

Ever since childhood, we have been bombarded with stories and beliefs that got stored in the reserves of our minds, and sadly some of the decisions we make today are based on unfounded beliefs. This book will help you do a mental excavation and seek out knowledge and wisdom that will enable you to grow and become a better and more fulfilled individual. However, true fulfillment can never be achieved by chasing other people's dreams, but by designing your own life goals based on who you truly are, which is critical to *"Finding Your Moment of Clarity."*

You will be truly amazed as you start to achieve new and better results by employing the concepts and ideas outlined in this book in everything you do. These are the same ideas used by inspiring leaders, self-made millionaires and big-time winners because when you control your thoughts, your thoughts control your reality and by reality, I mean how you feel and how you behave. If you think like a failure, you feel like a failure and behave like one too, because your thoughts reinforce self-perpetuating cycles.

Again, as long as you are going to think anyway, why not think great thoughts and get great results? Because negative chatter hampers our ability to focus, intensifies stress and takes us further away from our set goals. But when you have positive thoughts, you are able to cope better with stressful situations and reduce the harmful effects of stress on your body. Research shows that having a positive mental attitude will likely increase your life span as well as your psychological and physical well-being. It then becomes obvious that when you adopt positive thoughts, you embrace the opportunity to transform your life, the way you interact with others and the way you treat yourself. What do you have to lose?

So, sit back, hold on tight and get ready for your bravest journey into your future. You are about to experience a life-changing moment of clarity. Enjoy!

Thank You Adaku

PROLOGUE

Finding Your Moment Of Clarity Using Your Own Thoughts

By Michael Bart Mathews

T here's a survey in the United States that says; if you track 100 people starting even at the age of 25, do you have any idea what will happen to those men and women by the time they reach age 65? Those 100 people (at age 25) believe they are going to be successful. They are eager toward life. There is a certain sparkle in their eyes, an erectness to their carriage, and life seems like a pretty good interesting adventure to them. By the time they're 65:

1. 1 will be rich.
2. 4 will be financially independent.
3. 5 will still be working.
4. 54 will be broke and depending on others for life's necessities.
5. 36 will no longer be living

Only five out of 100 make the grade. Why do so many people fail? What happened to the sparkle in their eyes when they were 25? What has become of their dreams, hopes, the plans? Why is there such a significant disparity between what these people intended to do and what they actually accomplished?

Those were the words of Earl Nightingale.

STOP for a moment. Now think back to when you were age 25. Think about the many different personal relationships with different people from within different circles of life. Now in the present time (whatever your age is) think about how many of those same people (for whatever reason) is not currently making the grade by being financially independent. How come they don't have access to all the necessities that are available to every single one of us here on earth. What happened to the sparkle in their eyes? How come they did not make the grade?

If you happened to fall in the number one or number two category above and you are age 65, think about what you did differently that afforded you your current financial freedom. In most cases; the answer stems from the choices we made from our decisions of thought! If you are not age 65, based on where you are right now in life today, are you setting yourself up to be in the number one or number two categories above? With certainty, are your plans solid enough that you know you will make the grade?

IMAGINE while you are reading this book, in every chapter, you become aware of how to discover and harness your personal power within. Imagine you make the grade by taking a more balanced approach as you begin to get serious about *"Finding Your Moment of Clarity."* Think about building a strong, positive empowering introspective vision of how you see yourself transforming into the success that is your birthright. Think about giving yourself a truthful self-examination of your own thoughts, feelings, and actions that are holding you back from achievement.

Now imagine you have shredded those self-sabotaging, emotional baggage blockers from within your thoughts. You now can clearly see what it is that you want to accomplish, and you know how you will achieve it.

Think about and imagine how hard your retirement life might be if you do not do what others won't, so you can live and retire like millions don't. It's time to get serious and really begin thinking about which one of the above categories are you headed toward.

Imagine you have now embraced the thought leadership movement of making your paradigm shift toward *"Finding Your Moment of Clarity."* Imagine you know your why and you have begun seeking that "special specific something" that you most desire to achieve.

THINK ABOUT being better equipped at helping yourself to discover your own personal internal guiding light that is waiting, wanting, willing, ready and able to illuminate your journey with each step that you take. Think about walking your transformational journey within your thoughts. Imagine decluttering your self-imposed, mentally challenging, destructive habits. Only then, will you begin to brighten and change your new path with new success driven transformational habits.

Think about you are now a go-getter in life rather than remaining stagnant, and still sitting on the sidelines while the game of life passes you by. Imagine getting off the porch, and now you are running with the big dogs who all have a vision, goals, current dreams, and plans that lead to action.

Imagine feeling amazing and no longer frustrated when you begin to understand that EXCUSITIS is no longer a viable option. Would you agree that EXCUSITIS is another form of one not facing their fears, not believing that they are up to par or good enough for any number of reasons! EXCUSITIS (a form of low self-esteem & self-doubt) causes one to withdraw from growth, opportunities, social affairs, family events, and friends.

Think about EXCUSITIS being the number one reason people don't accomplish their goals, dreams, and desires. Think about how many times you said; I didn't do it because of blah, blah, blah. Think about why you make excuse after excuse for not taking action, rather than doing whatever it takes to accomplish "that special specific something?" No one really cares about the excuses. The high altitude and frequency level from your positive mental attitude makes all the difference in the world, wouldn't you agree?

You are already aware that winners never quit and quitters never win, aren't you? Think about the only way for you to actually fail is to give up and quit trying. Imagine becoming a winner, and you are no longer off your square or missing the bull's eye in the center of your target. Think about being on point and no longer walking around aimlessly or being a wondering generality! Wouldn't you rather become a meaningful specific, because you found your moment of clarity and you know exactly what you want in life? Wouldn't you?

Imagine and seriously think about the new you, always hitting the target (your goal) right in the bullseye, because you know your WHY [reason or purpose – goal or dream]. Imagine you are finally staying focused on achieving "that special specific something" that you most desire, regardless of any and all obstacles that will surely stand in your way from time to time!

Think about this question; are you clear on what your purpose is in this life? Your purpose or moment of mental clarity can also be identified as being your "heart's burning desire." Your WHY [reason or purpose - goal or dream] or your vision, is the most important factor on your journey toward success! Your WHY [reason or purpose - goal or dream] can be defined within the everyday thoughts that you think, the words that you speak, along with the actions that you take, and the people that you associate with. Your WHY is the most crucial factor that will determine your success!

Seriously think about and imagine you begin to purge and root out the negative people, the nay-sayers, the pessimist, and the conformist who all tell you that you can't do it. Now think about and imagine you have a new set of positive, thought leaders who believe and have faith in words and thoughts like: "let's not concentrate on how we can't accomplish this or that, let's focus and direct our thoughts and energy on how we can accomplish and achieve "that special specific something".

Seeking the answer to this question will be one of your life's bravest journey's that you will ever undertake! Imagine yourself stepping out of the dark shadows of mediocrity from holding yourself hostage from self-sabotaging, defeating thoughts. Imagine removing yourself from the doldrums of inactivity and stagnation.

Imagine yourself raising your mental antenna to its highest frequency level of thought leadership. Imagine yourself stepping into the energy filled, illuminating light of awareness and transformation. Imagine that you just grabbed the bull named opportunity by the horns, and rode your opportunity bull across the success line that surely awaits you.

Discovering your Why [reason or purpose - goal or dream] that enables you to do what you do comes from *Finding Your Moment of Clarity!*

Seriously think about what is holding you back from seeing through the thick, dense fog that impedes your vision from *Finding Your Moment of Clarity.* What is blocking you from visualizing and seeing your heart's burning desire?

> "Setting goals is the first step turning the invisible into the visible."
> -Tony Robbins

Are you still searching for those particular set of clues or keys that will unlock your positive power of thought, belief, feelings, and actions that generate results? Do you want to begin thinking with clarity, with the end result being achieving your vision? Imagine you are now thinking, feeling, and acting with confidence?

Do you want to take control of your emotions while experiencing your breakthrough after breakthrough feelings that you are doing "that special specific something" that the Universe has in store for you, and only you to accomplish? Do you want to learn or enhance the secrets of building better relationship capital with others?

IMAGINE having success in your personal life, as well as in your business relationships that are similar to the following story of the growth and development cycle of the Chinese bamboo tree. Read on and discover the many comparable lessons. Take a mental note of the obligations of the caretaker who planted the seed of the Chinese bamboo tree. He clearly knew and understood his Why [reason or purpose] that it took throughout the five-year growth cycle of the tree.

Remember, as you read the following story, imagine yourself being the seed planter and caretaker of your WHY [reason or purpose - goal or dream]. And most importantly, see yourself in your vision accomplishing "that special something" that you seek to achieve in your life.

THE STORY BEGINS:

Like any other plant, the growth of the Chinese bamboo tree needs fertile soil, ample water, sunshine and constant nurturing from a focused, and persistent caretaker. In the first year, there are no visual signs of growth above ground. The second, third and fourth years, there is still no visible signs of growth above ground, even though it has always received ample water, sunshine and constant nurturing from its caretaker.

During the fifth year of the growth and development cycle of the tree, a miraculous occurrence happens! The Chinese bamboo tree grows exponentially above ground, to an amazing eighty-feet-tall tree in just six weeks!

The question is, did the Chinese bamboo tree grow eighty-feet-tall in six weeks, or did it remain dormant for four years only to grow eighty-feet-tall in one year?

Or did the Chinese bamboo tree grow deep down beneath the topsoil, unseen to the human eye for the first four years, establishing strong, deep-seated roots, while building a solid foundation strong enough to hold up the next six weeks of exponential growth?

I think we all can agree, had the tree not developed a strong foundation underneath the soil it could not have been able to sustain its life as it grew above ground in six weeks. Our success is similar to the growth cycle of the Chinese bamboo tree.

> "There is one quality which one must possess to win, and that is definiteness of purpose, the knowledge of what one wants, and a burning desire to possess it."
> -Napoleon Hill

Now think about and imagine yourself experiencing the desired results from exponential growth that you seek, over a specified, predetermined length of time because you now have a realistic plan of action, just like the caretaker.

You must become the "seed planter and caretaker" of your own thoughts, your WHY, your goals, and your dreams. You must believe in yourself while going through your growth and personal development cycle if you really seek transformation and success in the area of your choosing.

The growth and development cycle of the Chinese bamboo tree teaches us several different lessons in comparison to personal growth and self-actualization cycles, which leads to transformational change and success. (1) How to be patient and persistent while having no visible growth above ground during the first through fourth years. (2) Keeping the necessary faith knowing that the tree will grow. (3) The perseverance needed to nurture (take action) the seed (your idea) and always keep going (one to five-year goals) and never giving up on achieving your heart's burning desire (your vision).

Imagine always viewing your life through the eyes of an optimist who knows, feels and believes that good things will happen now and in the future, just like the caretaker of the Chinese bamboo tree. Think about always seeing a positive outcome even though you're faced with adversity at different times along your journey.

Think about how amazing you will feel when you no longer think like a pessimist who feels or believes negative possibilities and or expects the worst possible outcome? Oh, what a relief!

> "A pessimist sees the difficulty in every opportunity; an optimist sees the opportunity in every difficulty."
> -Winston Churchill

William Arthur Ward - "The optimist lives on the peninsula of infinite possibilities; the pessimist is stranded on the island of perpetual indecision."

OPTIMIST – If you think that you can, then you can!

PESSIMIST – If you think that you can't, then you can't!

Turn to Chapter 1 and read about why we are here on earth. It's an introspective look within our own personal thoughts and belief systems, which has the power to make or break us using our own optimist or pessimist mindset.

To gain access to your free bonus gift, stop reading NOW! Go to www.tmeginc.com and claim your free bonus gift NOW; while they last! After you claim your gift, come back and continue on your life's bravest journey, while you are *"Finding Your Moment of Clarity."*

SECTION ONE

FINDING YOUR MOMENT OF CLARITY YOUR JOURNEY TO SELF-DISCOVERY

CHAPTER 1

WHY ARE WE HERE ON EARTH, AND WHAT IS OUR PURPOSE?

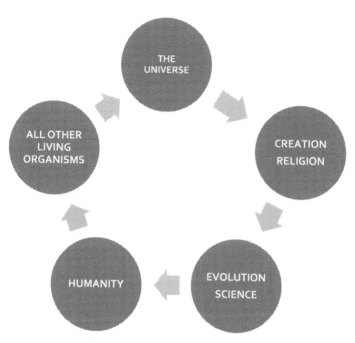

By Michael Bart Mathews

W hy are we here on earth and what is our reason or purpose for being here? How did the human race begin? What do you think about the following two theories regarding how the human race came into existence? As you read *"Finding Your Moment of Clarity,"* your answers will suddenly appear seemingly out of nowhere about why you are here on earth and what is your purpose. You will forever feel the light, awareness, energy, frequency, and vibrations of the Universe, while walking your bravest journey called everyday life.

1. Some followers believe in the Creation/Religion theory.
2. Other followers believe in the Evolution/Science theory.

Whether you believe in Creationism/Religion or Evolution/ Science, the fact remains that we are all here on earth today as living, intelligent human beings. Our mission, if we choose to accept it, is to discover what our purpose here on earth is while we walk our bravest journey called everyday life.

Understanding your WHY [reason or purpose - goal or dream] will bring about that needed force of positive mental clarity and direction necessary for personal growth and development toward achievement.

The Universe is full of many different sources of powerful energy, frequencies, and vibrations. We (you and I) are also a form of energy that uses fuel (air, food & water) to go about our daily tasks. Our brains also require mind food for thought. If you don't feed your mind, it shall waste away! Many Universal laws have helped millions of people to find their WHY [reason or purpose – goal or dream].

The law of energy-energy is everything. The law of attraction-we become what we think about. The law of abundance-prosperity, not scarcity. The law of cause and effect; meaning whatever you send into the universe will come back.

What I mean by success covers a broad spectrum of different meanings. Success starts with personal development and how harmoniously we get along in life with others. Question; how can you expect to achieve martial, spiritual, personal, business, athletic or financial success if you don't understand your WHY [reason or purpose - goal or dream] and how to get along with others in life?

The Universal laws that will be discussed in the following chapters are priceless, and you cannot purchase them with all the money in the world. These Universal laws can cause a profound paradigm shift for positive transformation. You have the ability to live a more self-satisfying, peaceful, well rounded, successfully balanced lifestyle, that you choose for yourself. If you don't know where you're going, how will you know when you get there? You are the person who must dig deep down within yourself, while you are *"Finding Your Moment of Clarity"* as you discover your WHY [reason or purpose - goal or dream].

It's up to you to believe that it is possible to achieve a higher level of existence here on earth. Why are we here on earth and what is our Why [reason or purpose - goal or dream]? We could have been a bird, a tree, a shark or whale, a dog or a cat. Instead, we are at the top of the food chain being human! Don't let that power go to waste.

> *"The prime purpose in this life is to help others. And if you can't help them, at least don't hurt them."*
> -Dalai Lama

The Universal laws are here to assist us in finding our true purpose in life. Only if we seek to do so! Energy is levitating invisibly in the atmosphere standing by for our antennas to level up and tap into the most-high frequency of mental thought.

You have the power to transform your life. The principal centered Universal laws are meant for you to interpret for yourselves while *"Finding Your Moment of Clarity."* They are designed to encourage you to take a stroll through your mind, enabling you the opportunity to reintroduce your new self to the old person that you left behind, each and every time you look into the mirror of transformation.

Imagine gaining a better understanding of the natural energy of the Universe from using the power of your positive thoughts. Think about how your thoughts are designed to help you transform how you think, act and feel about where you are today in life and where you want to go in the future. The Universal laws will assist you in *"Finding Your Moment of Clarity,"* specifically defining where it is that you want to go in life, as you discover your heart's burning desire, your WHY [reason or purpose – goal or dream].

I know you have been blessed to have many achievements and successes in your lifetime. Do you also feel that there is more in this Universe for you to experience and achieve? I know you are a multi-tasker. I know you have a full plate every day with things to do, places to go, people to see.

STOP! Find a quiet place where you will not be interrupted for about 15 minutes. Turn off your mobile phone and close your eyes. Mentally take a real hard look at yourself in your present state today, right now at this very moment. You know how you currently feel while having both feet standing firmly on first base (whatever your profession is). Now look at home plate (a promotion or entrepreneurship), how are you going to get there if you don't take your foot off first base (current situation)? You have second base, third base, and home plate directly in your line of sight (short, medium, and long-term goals). The only thing that's holding you back is your lack of belief and not taking action (lack of vision). In other words, you must swing until you hit, regardless of how many times you strike out!

In life, you must learn how to visualize yourself swinging until you hit (trying one idea after another) and then reaching first base. Next, moving on to second base (results from setting another goal), on to third base (more results from setting another goal), and crossing home plate, scoring (achieving the goals). Now feel the excitement and pleasure of achievement because you ran around the bases in the game of life, by taking action and accomplishing one goal at a time or swinging until you hit.

Swing (taking action), until you hit simply means that you will not hit every pitch out of the park, or achieve every goal that you set unless you quit. Sometimes you will strike out (fail). Batter-up! Next inning, swing (take action) hit the pitch (goal) high over (back-back-back, hey-hey) the center field fence for a grand-slam home run (achievement of goal)! Standing in the batter's box in a game of baseball, compared to waking up bright and early every day in the game of life, never stop swinging until you hit your goals!

Now close your eyes and time travel back when you were standing in the batter's box at home plate. You had two choices; the 1st choice was to let every ball (idea, goal or dream) fly past you while you stood there watching and wishing. 2nd choice was to take action and swing until you hit because you clearly defined your WHY [reason or purpose - goal or dream] long before you stepped into the batter's box of life. By swinging until you hit, you were no longer stuck in life and the feeling of procrastination and failure no longer consumed and paralyzed your forward moving creative thoughts toward change and success.

The desire for success using a positive change of thought, feelings and actions by way of personal growth and development must out way procrastination, negativity (pessimism) and the fear of failure, bar none!

We all are here on earth to find and complete our individual and unique purpose driven life. The Universe has put on our shoulders, a great humanitarian burden of responsibility for the greater good of mankind and the existence of the human race.

No one has the same journey as we travel across time and space from one generation to the next! Thoughts are intangible frequencies that guide our every day to day feelings and actions. Our thoughts are snapshots of our visions. Our frequency of positive thoughts, aligned with clarity of goals, followed by the correct type of (energy) and action, equals all the life-changing vibrations of motivation. Which collectively have the capacity to deliver positive results. The life-changing power of motivation is described in Chapter 2 by my friend Marja Katajisto. Have your pen and paper handy and write down your new ideas that come to mind from Marja's contribution.

THE LIFE CHANGING POWER OF MOTIVATION

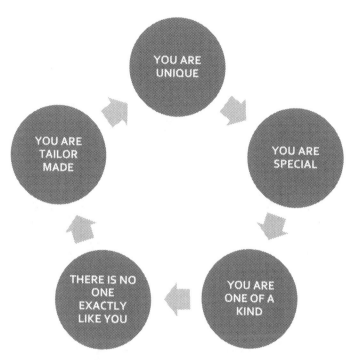

Allow me, to introduce you, to my good friend, Marja Katajisto
By Marja Katajisto

L et me begin by saying, that you, my dear sister or brother, are one of a kind in this Universe - unique and so very, very special. There is no one like you, and there never will be anyone exactly like you. Not even if you were to be cloned. Not even if you have an identical twin.

THE WORLD NEEDS YOUR BRILLIANCE

Besides being the delightfully brilliant sum of billions of cells, with their own unique code which we merely call the "genetics," we also are sculpted and polished by different flavors of times and continuously varying circumstances.

The multitude of your life experiences along the way are spiced up by all the people touching your daily life. Your parents, siblings and the extended family, friends, acquaintances, teachers, bosses, priests and strangers... they all contribute.

You simply are modified by everything living and even by the past legacies. Their influence comes from their teachings, beliefs, opinions and by the examples they set. They assist in forming and designing an individual called by your name. You have many talents, those unseen, and those already discovered, all have mental or physical strength, unique personal features and even things that we wrongly call "shortcomings." One must conclude that all these are ingredients interconnected with the heavy millstones of life.

Every living moment, whether a success story or a hardship experience has meaning. Every person past or present from our daily strives, in the form of a strict teacher or a lost loved one, has built you up for your ultimate mission in this life. The windmill of life never stops turning. It wants to enable you to bake the cakes that you were sent here to bake. Because if you don't bake them, no one else ever will. And that would be an unfortunate loss for our times. So, thank you for sharing your wonderful energy and light with us!

You are here for a reason. For all of us, there is a plan. You have a personal mission package, that's tailor-made to perfectly fit your unique set of talents and features. The area of your personal talents gives hints about the direction in which your outstanding contributions can help create change. Find your passions! Your soul food!

Rewarding and wonderfully inspiring projects are waiting for you!! Exactly those tasks, which you will find fulfilling, are offering a multitude of opportunities. It will not all be bliss or a graceful dance on a bed of roses, that's for sure. What it will be, is the treasure map to a happy, balanced and meaningful life. To that place where one lives and breathes his or her strengths and passions.

My theory is that all those feeling hopelessness in this world, never seriously sought after their true mission-tasks. As a result, they are now not fulfilling their designated responsibilities. Their lives might feel unhappy and without a deeper purpose. Such people are like raw diamonds – yes, mined and found - but left in the rough, uncut and unpolished state of existence. Their splendid beauty and value will stay unrecognized, and they will never arrive at the home of their dreams. I can imagine that emptiness and frustration is very likely present in their daily lives. Their fullest contribution to this world will not take place, and the joy of life remains a rare moment. Very sad and what a loss!

I wonder if you too have come to realize that quite often the modest street singers in rags actually sign and play better than many others seen on exclusive stages in front of cheering audiences. Also, I have met highly educated experts, who now are searching for food behind small restaurants. They search for food in smelly bins, while eating hand to mouth! That's just so very, very sad and wrong in this world of abundance.

No matter what you are doing in life, you are always moving forward at the pace and direction of your own choice. Never reversing, because you can't! Life happens now, and it is always moving forward. Which is the reason why "NOW" is the most important moment. It is the only time frame you can be certain you are doing everything "NOW" as you walk your journey of *"Finding Your Moment of Clarity"*!

To make this "NOW" matter and unleash its fullest reward and potential, a master plan-map is needed:

1. My goal, what do I want to achieve?
2. Why? What's in it for me?
3. Are my answers to the above questions really honest?

Hidden in the answers to those very important questions, lies the amazing sparkle of motivation.

THE MAGIC OF MOTIVATION

What actually is motivation? It doesn't have a form, color or smell. It is invisible and intangible, yet an absolute necessity for everything in this life under the titles "change" and "improvement." Without motivation nothing new would ever be created, everything would stay the same.

A certain amount of motivation had to take place for you to sit down and read this great educational book *"Finding Your Moment of Clarity,"* written by my dear friend, Michael Bart Mathews, "Big Mike." The reasoning behind Big Mike's motivation might have been his want and need to create this product, while enlisting the talents and help from every co-author, including me!

As the long history of mankind proves that curious and creative minds are the very best experts in finding motivation, some people will find a way to move mountains. They are able to bring themselves to the deepest sources of unwavering world changing motivation! Sometimes they admirably manage to bring many others with them to the source of motivation because they took action!

So many modern-day conformities which today, we take too easily as a given right or privilege, were not too long ago just crazy ideas by even crazier people. Thank God for their goals and motivation! Without them, we would still wash all the laundry by hand in wells and lakes. Without any complaint, we would also make a two-week boat trip to reach the USA from Europe. Just to name two examples of wonderful and life-improving innovations, which "motivation" has proudly given birth to. The washing machine and the airplane.

The word "motivation" sounds very serious. It is a term easily thrown into discussions, especially in the field of coaching. Why? Because it sounds so "grounded," wise and logical! But do we really understand its true meaning along with its mission in the big picture of cause and effect? Do we care to remember what brings motivation into life? How fragile and short-lived an outbound burst, or wave of motivation can be? It is that strong magnet placed a bit further into your future. It is what is attracting you and motivating you to keep pushing forward.

Actually, while mulling over this change-making concept of "motivation," I have quite fallen in love with its raw and beautiful power. Just think, it's clean, it's natural, and it's even a renewable resource! There is an abundance of it! Yes, in you, my friend and also in me, and in every living soul. You are a transformational Power House! Yes, just go and ignite your flame of Motivation! I say, "move forward!". It is the fuel of fuels which drives you all the way to your goals, both big and small. Motivation. The fuel of all fuels, I say.

THE VITAL COMPONENT

But wait! "Something is missing," you say, and you would be right. Because motivation never lives alone. It can only coexist with goals, and the two are very tight-knit. You see, only the goal can light up the flame of your motivation which will push you through tough times. With a high level of motivation, you will be resourceful, inventive, strong and resilient in front of whatever challenges you may meet along the way. There can't be motivation without a goal.

Now you see how important it is to have a clear understanding of your big and small goals. Seeing them *"Finding Your Moment of Clarity"* in your mind's horizon brings you willpower, focus, and determination. Having clarity about your direction and destination makes you run like a train on straight rails from beginning to accomplishment. Goals and motivation, one creates the other.

Your first task is to make sure that the goals you have chosen are the correct ones. Are they truly yours? Or someone else's? Are your goals true and authentic? Motivating? Ask yourself "is this really what I want?" And if the answer is "yes" that will automatically ignite your motivation. Which means that your journey towards your target, close or distant, has immediately started. Your creative project-manager-mind starts to build up a route or path towards your goal. Following the mission path will eventually bring you to success.

This wonderful method allows you to see the milestones and the whole path to your goals. Milestones between now and then play an important role, just as reaching them will keep you hungry and motivated. They offer a self-feeding effect while seeking out the task.

Motivation pushes you to think if plans B and C are needed. Maybe even a plan D? Which are the required processes? Are there some deadlines or timing-issues included? Do you need help? What can possibly go wrong? How can you be prepared, and avoid mistakes and surprises? You will find the answers to every important question once the motivation is ignited.

Yes, a process-train like this will eventually bring you to your target, the desired destination. The ticket counter is open 24/7. You will find it in the lively main street of your mind. Why not buy a ticket right "NOW"? Get the journey started on the road to *"Finding Your Moment of Clarity."* This is the perfect moment to whisk in that good old saying: "If there is a will, there is a way."

This saying has lived a long time, from numerous past generations up to our modern days. Not because it is witty, but only because it is the absolute truth. Believe in it, and you will never have a use for the word "excuse" anymore. You have the power of self-motivation. Why would anyone choose not to use such a power-tool? One is able to make a difference. That one, being you, and you, and you. If everyone believes it, the magic of motivation will create miracles beyond our wildest dreams. When you want something strong enough, you will always find a way forward towards whatever it is you wish to have or achieve.

In this context, water drips into my mind. How it always finds its way down and through to the lakes and oceans from the highest mountains. Through the sand and soil, and those multiple layers of past times, and down to the groundwater. It even makes its way through man-made constructions, such as walls, roofs, floors, and dams.

Water, like motivation, needs to adapt. It can change from a liquid to a gas or a solid. It represents the character of motivation so very well. Relentless and resourceful. It can't be destroyed. It only changes form in order to adapt! Quitting is simply not an option.

MOTIVATION MAKES IT POSSIBLE

Without a doubt, this amazingly beautiful, logic and ingenious concept of life is a masterpiece without compare. In existence, a "standstill" moment has never occurred, there always was and always will be a follow-up. No matter what challenges our civilization throws at mother nature, she always has an answer.

Something happens, and we would be naive to think that the final outcome somehow is in our hands. We truly are guests and passengers in this adventure called life, and we have to respect it. Nevertheless, it is important to remember that each and every one of us is equipped to assist and give a hand in various ways.

Daily, I think about our brilliance, the power to create. To be empathetic and loving, to make wise decisions, as well as to be responsible and accountable. They all are conscious choices. If you think about it, to have powers of that magnitude is actually overwhelming. A massive tsunami of motivation to do good deeds should be a natural product of such powers, but we humans are highly complicated creatures. In us, millions of different feelings and variables are in constant centrifuge.

Every decision we make is a new one because the staging of the moment is always a new one as well. Everything is connected, and thus when one area changes or is in stress, all other areas are also affected. It is a holistic system and thus impossible to be described in its every detail.

Even the strongest motivation can suffer a temperature-drop if other matters around it are not (temporarily) aligned with the main-efforts. In those situations, one's priorities have to be focused elsewhere for the sake of general good.

When the motivator is an external factor (extrinsic), instead of a reason that comes from your inside (intrinsic) there is a bigger risk of losing the "battle spirit." At such moments, one hopes that friends and family can offer all-saving support. Personally, I have experienced the incredible power of coaching at such moments.

A good coach not only can provide you with tools to fight forward, but also brings a new, bright shining light on your distant goal or dreams. *"Finding Your Moment of Clarity"* allows you to become re-motivated and the goals become visible again. By tapping into that vision, that new state of life will eventually take place, step by step.

CATCH THE OPPORTUNITIES!

When the author of this book, my dear friend, Mr. Michael Bart Mathews kindly approached me and asked whether I would want to appear as a guest-writer in his newest book, I was thrilled! What an honor! Of course, I would! I can promise you, my dear readers, that I was so very, very <u>motivated</u>! What an opportunity! Thank you very much, Big Mike!

Now my humble wish is that with my input, I have succeeded in reminding you about the essential ingredients of success, without any complication.

Here below is a short summary:

- Visions innovative ideas and dreams create goals.
- Goals bring light to mid-way milestones and needed systems.
- Step-by-step plans clarify the direction and the first right moves.

- Motivation is the fuel that keeps things moving! Stay motivated! Find your reason "why"?

Kindly be encouraged dear reader to fully appreciate the great powers of change-making, which are irreversibly installed in our very beings. All we have to do is just embrace them, enhance them and keep them in action. Everything is possible when you are motivated!

Mr. Michael Bart Mathews and his wonderful wife Robbie are amazing people, and I am very proud to be called their friend! They both are doing very important work in bringing fantastic money-management tools to people who desperately need them. I could not be prouder of them.

I want to wish them both the very best of luck and Godspeed to all of your endeavors. Keep the fire of motivation burning in your bellies!

Thank You Marja

CHAPTER 3

DO YOU KNOW WHERE YOUR THOUGHTS ARE

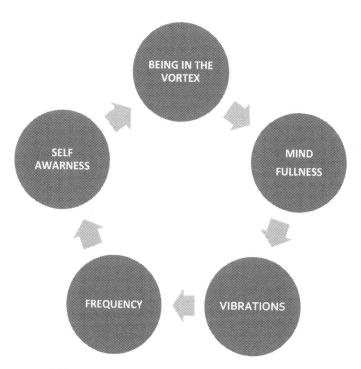

Allow me, to introduce you, to my good friend, Natalie M. Bonomo
By Natalie M. Bonomo

PRACTICE MINDFULNESS TO GET INTO THE VORTEX

Y ou may be asking yourself, is this vortex way of thinking really possible? Does being in the vortex really help to attract the life you desire? Absolutely! With the law of attraction, what you think about, you bring about. Thoughts affect feelings which affect your vibration, and your vibration works like a magnet attracting things to you. Therefore, by raising your vibration, you allow yourself to enter the vortex. In the vortex, you attract your desires, and by doing so, you improve your life exponentially!

> *"Being in the Vortex means you're at one with who you really are, you're feeling fab, and in vibrational alignment with your desires."*
> *-Abraham Hicks*

If you are at all wondering if this vortex concept really exists, consider your own thought patterns throughout your life. Has there ever been a period where you felt a little odd, out of balance, disconnected, or as though you were just drifting along, following the sheep, all going in the same direction? Have you ever experienced a feeling of knowing you needed to make a change, but couldn't pinpoint how to go about doing it?

In a more extreme situation, perhaps you had several things out of balance at one time and thought to yourself, as strange as this may have sounded, my life has nothing to do with me. Your only hope was that one day you would awaken from this bizarre dream, and step into a new life overflowing with purpose, balance, and overall well-being. These low periods in life are representative of being out of the vortex.

To understand what it means to be "in" or "out" of the vortex, as described in the introduction in the words of Abraham Hicks, recall a time in your life when it felt like you were treading water, swimming upstream, or stuck in an eddy. You may recall instances of repeating the same dreadful relationship over and over but with different partners; foregoing financial troubles; landing and leaving undesired employment time after time or having a family or social fall-out. Choose a time, whatever comes to mind for you, that you clearly knew you were out of balance, "out" of the vortex, and things were not going according to plan. Make a mental note of this out-of- the-vortex experience as it will be used later in doing an autopsy of the thinking that got you there. This will also assist you in *"Finding Your Moment of Clarity."*

Now, let's focus on what it means to be "in" the vortex. You often hear sports references when someone was "in the zone" and played a flawless game, making it look effortless. Clearly, they were in the vortex. What occasion stands out in your mind that made you feel in the zone? Think of an event when a surge of energy engulfed your mind, body, and soul and became the decision-making driver, steering you right into the heart of the current while allowing you to operate at full capacity with confidence and ease.

In that event or situation, you were undoubtedly in the vortex. Other examples may include giving a stellar speech or performing a flawless solo and receiving a standing ovation or nailing an interview and landing that dream job. Focus on a particular event or experience when you were clearly in the zone or in the vortex, savor that moment and how it felt, and make a mental note of this situation or event as it will be used a little later in this section.

Having identified at least one "in" and one "out" of the vortex experience, let's now dissect the root cause of both situations and/or events – from your thinking! We get what we think about, period. Whether we want it or not, we attract what we focus on, good and bad. Our thoughts are magnetic and based on the frequency (vibration) of our thoughts, we attract a vibrational match. Therefore, by the universal law of attraction, we create our reality.

Whether or not our thoughts are positive or negative determines the outcome of the experience we manifest. How do we do this? Imagine tuning a radio station from one channel to the next. You are changing the frequency each time a different station plays. The same is true with your thoughts. You are literally tuning to a frequency or vibration that matches the level of your thoughts. Understanding the law of attraction, you can tune your vibration to match the level of the outcome you desire, be it positive (high vibration) or negative (low vibration).

To prove this law of attraction is true, think about the negative Nellies you know. These are the continuous complainers who are rarely happy about anything. Can you see any examples of where they may be attracting their own misery, where their negative, low vibrational thoughts lead to negative behaviors, words, and actions which in turn lead to outcomes that are also negative? Have you ever been sitting next to a person like this and, whether you knew them or not, you could feel their negative energy desecrating the air around them? That toxic, low vibrational energy, unfortunately, can spread like wildfire and be witnessed across various facets of their lives as proof that they have attracted the inevitable consequences of their vibration.

Contrarily, do you know someone who is an eternal optimist, upbeat, confident, thoughtful, and kind? They are focused on seeing the bright side of things and has an abundance of great things happening in their life? Have you noticed how when they step into a room, the energy increases? You may see them as financially well-off, enjoying their work and family, doing what they love, and things come easily to them. Whether or not they are aware of it, they are in the vortex. And they are using their high vibration energy to attract what they desire. Odds are they understand the importance of *"Finding Your Moment of Clarity."*

Understanding that you deliberately create your experiences through your thoughts. Let's examine the situations and events from your life where you tuned into a particular frequency. Reflect, for a moment, on the situation or event in which you were out of the vortex or in a place of low vibration. What kinds of thoughts led you to that experience?

Were you anticipating the outcome being positive or negative? Did you have self-doubt or faith in achieving the desired end result? Were your thoughts coming from a place of lack? Did you maybe see signs of concern before heading down that path or arriving at the point of a less-than-desirable result? Take a moment to reflect on what station or frequency was playing in your mind at that time. Would you say it was one of high or low vibration?

If you were to re-play your self-talk from that period of time, would you approve of how you were speaking to yourself, find it nurturing, encouraging, or offensive? How about your emotional guidance system (your gut feelings), were you paying attention to them and following the vibration leading up to the event or situation? If not, do you feel the outcome may have been different had you paid attention? Do not dwell on any negative or low energy feelings surrounding the event or situation as that will certainly keep you out of the vortex. The intention of this exercise is merely to illustrate how events or situations are manifested by our thought vibration. And we have an emotional guidance system telling us whether or not what we are attracting is good or bad for us based on how it feels.

Now, switch to the time you recalled as being in the vortex (high vibration). How were you thinking and feeling prior to that situation or event? Were you envisioning a positive or negative outcome? Did you have self-doubt or faith in achieving the desired end result? Reflect for a moment on the station or frequency to which you were tuned. Was it one of high or low vibration? Was your self-dialogue positive and encouraging leading up to the event or situation? What was your emotional guidance system telling you at the time?

Before the situation or event, did you feel light or heavy about what was happening? As you answer these questions, jot down a few notes to refer to as you dissect and fine-tune your thought process. Becoming mindful of your thoughts, you can learn to train your mind to this frequency on a regular basis. By revisiting this high vibration experience, you will not only raise your current vibration by reliving the wonderfulness of it, but you will also re-engage and activate the in-the-vortex mindset that got you there in the first place and cultivate more wonderful high vibration experiences.

With careful dissection of your thoughts leading up to these two different events, your mental autopsies will reveal evidence of your thought patterns that led you to the results of each. These autopsies can teach you a valuable lesson on what type of mental programming you can use to create the results you desire from here forward. They can also help you to recognize when you are heading down a thought path that is not in the vortex or vibrating to a positive frequency. Therefore, it is not likely to yield a positive outcome or that which you desire.

Training your mind to a positive frequency takes practice to become good at it. It includes moment to moment work as well as positive rituals. Mindfulness is part of the moment to moment work. It's aware of the thoughts that come and go, noticing the quality of them, which ones are of high vibration and healthy thoughts. And which ones are of low vibration and negative thoughts that should be recognized and dismissed without attaching feelings or energy to them.

To better understand what it means to be mindful of your thoughts, imagine yourself watching your favorite television program and being interrupted by a commercial. Think of the commercial as a lower vibration thought. Commercials typically are a nuisance. You may or may not hear them, and you let them pass and then return to your program. Similarly, lower vibration thoughts (commercials) randomly appear. As with commercials, you can train your mind to recognize these out-of-the-vortex thoughts and allow them to pass through without giving them your full attention, and quickly change the channel back to a positive frequency of thought.

As you place your focus on something you desire, do so from a place of true appreciation. Bask in what you love about the subject. For example, if you desire money, a partner, a new car or house, simply ponder how delightful and life-enhancing it would be to have any of these things. Be careful not to simultaneously go about your thoughts from a place of lack. You cannot be thinking, I want a new house, but it's too expensive. I would love to be wealthy, but I have too much debt.

Thoughts of lack vibrate at a lower frequency and attract similar thoughts which then become your point of attraction. Instead, think of the joy or benefits that the subject adds to your life. It is impossible to remain in the vortex one hundred percent of the time. With practice, being mindful helps trigger when to gently dismiss negative thoughts and return to a place of being in the vortex.

According to Abraham Hicks, our chances of attracting that which we desire intensify the longer and the higher the level of the frequency, we remain in the vortex. This brings us to the idea of rituals. What better way to start and close your day than to begin and end with positive affirmations, gratitude, meditation or prayer! Practicing any or all of these daily rituals is a beautiful way to set your expectations for the day and attract more of what you desire.

Furthermore, according to Abraham Hicks, when you maintain your focus on a pure thought for 17 seconds, the law of attraction begins to respond and join that thought with similar thoughts of a matching vibration. Extend your focus for as long as 68 seconds on that thought, and the vibration becomes strong enough to activate physical manifestation. It is likely that positive affirmations, gratitude, meditation or prayer could take you at least 17 seconds. You can use this technique to your benefit or detriment. Being mindful of your thoughts is the key.

Going forward, use what you learned from the results of your mental autopsies about tuning your thoughts to a higher vibration as you begin to examine and guide your moment to moment thoughts. Begin with small steps, noticing when you break away from positive thinking; then nudge yourself back into positive thought. Next, take it a step further. Examine your self-talk, words, behaviors, and actions and evaluate each on a regular basis. With practice, as you minimize occurrences of being out of the vortex and increase opportunities for high vibration thoughts, you will make way for a vibrant, thriving, joyful existence.

You will discover the secret to living your life to the fullest. Adapting to a mindset of being in the vortex, you will never again drift aimlessly through the vicissitudes of life. You will soar like an eagle over the peaks and valleys. You will appreciate the entire breathtaking journey. You will understand that *"Finding Your Moment of Clarity"* while living with a clear focus and destination in mind, all as a result of the simple shifting of your thinking to a place dominated by the power of positivity.

Adapting to a lifestyle of being mindful, you'll become quite a pro at knowing when you are "in" or "out" of the vortex and you'll be able to make an adjustment upon recognizing a "momentary vibrational relapse" (being out the vortex, reverting to your old way of thinking), and then redirect yourself back into the vortex. In fact, you will also begin to recognize within the company you keep, who else is practicing this concept of being in the vortex, and who is not.

It will become blatantly obvious to you when you see and hear something that is out of vibrational alignment from your place of positivity (high vibration), that you have transformed your thinking and have learned to be mindful of your thoughts, self-talk, feelings, behaviors, words, and actions.

The benefits of in-the-vortex thinking are innumerable, and the better you get at practicing high vibration thoughts, the faster you reap the rewards. Aside from feeling good and attracting the results you desire, you will attract others who are aligned with your way of thinking. You will be increasingly surrounding yourself with like-minded individuals who are living their lives with clarity, purpose, and balance. Your life will flourish, becoming more balanced, meaningful, purposeful, and prosper what is already good to an infinite level of fulfillment.

Without a single trace of the "sheep" mentality that once riddled your life, you will lead others by example. Challenging yourself to remain in balance, inspired by your potential and the opportunities materializing around you, you will seek excellence in everything you do and truly become an on-purpose person.

Great things beyond your expectations will happen to you and to others because of you. Being in the vortex, you will radiate a glow that shines onto others, improving their lives through the ripple effect. You'll wake up in the morning, see a new you, and recognize a transformation has occurred. You'll begin your day feeling energized, grateful to be alive, and thankful for the amazing countless blessings in your life.

You will become inspired by all that is good in and with the world and find ways to contribute to making positive improvements. You will seek and discover the best in everyone and everything. A sense of sincere appreciation will be gained from things that went unnoticed before. Such as the feel of the rain, the sound of the wind, laughter, or the reflection on the water as they are magnified with endless beauty. Your focus will lean toward being connected to something greater than yourself, living with gratitude for the abundance and synchronicity you attract. You will experience being an instrument of peace and appreciating obstacles or bumps in the road as they too are blessings.

You will know you are in the vortex when your lifestyle is focused on how you can serve others or lift someone up. Your actions, words, and thoughts will come from a place of love. You will plant seeds of kindness wherever you go. Gratitude, love, joy, and peace will intertwine to form your compass and illuminate your path opening new doors. How humbling it will be to see how far you've come and what you've overcome, to be your new best self.

Your life will align with the vibration of peace and harmony, and your actions will support the changes you wish to see in the world. As any unhealthy habits disintegrate, they will be replaced with more positive practices that are aligned with your values. There will be a reason behind your every deliberate action, one that is clearly connected to and driven from your source or universal guidance.

As you learn to marinate your thoughts in all that is positive and dream big, your mind will expand and explode with goals, dreams, and aspirations. Through the law of attraction, you will invite the answers you seek to the forefront of your mind, and then listen and wait quietly. Signs will be revealed, and your emotional guidance system will nudge you to act. It is important to recognize that these messages and signs come as gifts from the universe, and taking action is a way of saying thank you for this guidance. Each and every time you take action when gifted with this guidance, greater moments of *Finding Your Moments of Clarity* will follow.

Like a beacon of light, you will ascend to greater heights, overcome what you may have once thought were insurmountable obstacles and find your wishes fulfilled. Living your dreams, you will remain humble in faith and with gratitude, and continue to be blessed by the universe. You will be soaring like an eagle with grace and beauty, poised, focused and with purpose. In an epiphany, a true moment of clarity and awakening, you will fully understand the impact of your mental paradigm shift and realize that your life has everything to do with you, and it's extraordinary!

Thank You Natalie

CHAPTER 4

STINKIN THINKIN

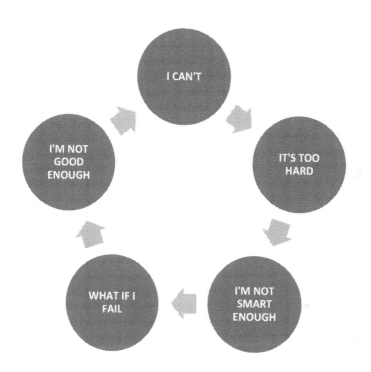

By Michael Bart Mathews

T he Cambridge dictionary defines stinkin thinkin as: "A bad way of thinking that makes you believe you will fail, that bad things will happen to you, or that you are not a very good person."

Is that inner voice inside of your head sometimes called "stinkin thinkin" talking you into thinking, feeling, and acting like the Grinch who stole Christmas or a bah-humbug scrooge, or Mr. Potter in It's a Wonderful Life? Giving yourself a checkup from the neck up, using positive thoughts to help you discover your moment of clarity is extremely essential for growth, self-help and personal development.

Stinkin thinkin can seep into our minds from various ways throughout our entire life, minute by minute. It keeps us out of the vortex. Watching television for hours upon hours can negatively fill up our mind with thoughts of injustice, negativity, sorrow, despair, and defeat. The political jargon between politicians, wars, disruption within communities all can keep those who stayed glued to watching television, disengaged from practicing, self-actualization, personal growth and development along with self-improvement activities.

> "Every day we need a checkup from the neck up, to avoid stinkin thinkin and the hardening of the attitudes."
> -Zig Ziglar

We are a sum total of our thoughts; meaning garbage in, garbage out! That little voice inside of our heads needs a constant daily prescribed check-up from the neck-up dose of positive thinking. When you seem to be mentally knocked off of your positive square, give yourself a much-needed checkup from the neck up and change your stinkin thinkin!

Become your biggest and loudest personal growth and development cheerleader for self-change. Give yourself a much needed, uplifting, power-packed, energy filled, prescribed dose of personal praise filled with positive affirmations. See yourself as who you want to become, long before you arrive. When sadness darkens your doorstep, visualize yourself being happy (use Meditation & Laughter Yoga techniques) as you begin to think happy thoughts.

You can transform yourself into a new, invigorating person, with a breath of positive fresh air. You can tap into and use the power of your mind by changing negative thoughts of stinkin thinkin and feelings into positive thoughts and happy, new feelings.

Improving work-balance and life-balance while *"Finding Your Moment of Clarity"* can also be transformed by changing your mindset. Trust the signals coming from the changing of emotions. That's a sign that your internal guidance system is telling you something. It's ok if they don't balance out equally all the time. Sometimes, one side requires more focus than the other side. No one is responsible for your happiness but you!

The thoughts that we think can play various amounts of sly, slick and wicked tricks of mental deceit and deception within our minds. The job at hand is to develop, safeguard against and protect that positive inner voice in your head. Never let negative energy, thoughts, feelings, and emotions hang around long. If they do hang around long enough, you might seem like you are sinking deep into the abyss, or down inside of an endless black hole of disparity. Learning and understanding about being in or being out of the vortex are so essential here, as my good friend and contributing author, Natalie shared with you.

As sure as the light shines brightly on a warm summer day, you have the power to be mentally strong, and morally straight. Use your positive thoughts like a lucky charm or a good luck four-leaf clover. Allow the magic of the Universe to transform the way you think, act and feel while you discover your home life-balance and also maintain the proper work-life balance!

Remember, the people who you surround yourself with, (circle of influence) has the ability to affect how you think, act and feel. Always guard against negative conversations (stinkin thinkin) from others! Protect your positive mental attitude.

"Never argue with stupid people, they will drag you down to their level and beat you with experience." – Mark Twain

CHAPTER 5

FOOD FOR THOUGHT

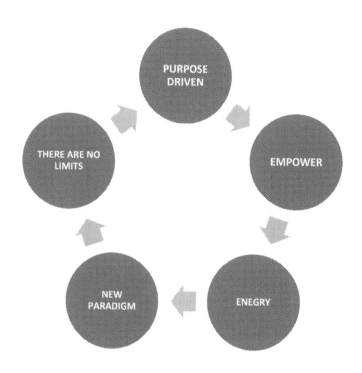

Allow me, to introduce you to my wife, Robbie Mathews
By Robbie Mathews

We all know that change and success will come in many different shapes, sizes, forms, and fashions. Change and success for one person is different for another. Have you seriously thought about why some people succeed while others fail? In reality, there is rarely no success without failure. So, why do some people keep on failing without achieving the level of success that they are capable of reaching? And why do some people succeed regardless of their circumstances?

They fail because they have not yet found their WHY (reason or purpose). In other words, they are not purpose-driven. There are numerous reasons for this that I will explore below. In your quest to find your moment of clarity, you will need to examine the reasons for what may be holding you back or what is empowering you to keep driving forward.

Reason #1 – Nature or Nurture - from birth, some people are born with the proverbial silver spoon in their mouths. They are referred to as trust fund babies. They are blessed to inherit sizable amounts of generational wealth (old money) because of the success of their generous benefactor. They go to the best schools and grow up discussing financial matters around the dinner table. Their parents are business owners. They deliberately groom their children to take over the family business or encourage them to start a business of their own. Their education also affords them the opportunity to get that high paying corporate job with all the perks. Even with all these advantages, some of them still fail in life.

However, others are born into less fortunate conditions beyond their control. They were born into the total opposite set of circumstances. They were born into poverty and did not come from generational wealth. Financial matters were never discussed at the dinner

> "If you were born poor, it's not your mistake, if you die poor, it's your mistake".
> -Bill Gates

table or in school. They did not go to the best of schools, and in some cases, they were the first in their family to attend college. Their parents weren't business owners and struggled to make ends meet. They had no trust fund. They had to hustle to make a living. Many born into these circumstances conform to mediocrity while never breaking the cycle of poverty or changing the status quo. While many others become successful in life, despite their disadvantages. It requires that they make a new paradigm shift to reach beyond their external surroundings. They find their why their reason or purpose to overcome their limitations. What about you?

Reason #2 – Fortune or Curse - regardless of the circumstances of your birth, what would you do if you either won the lottery or struck it rich at the casino or riverboat? How would you use the money? Would you seek guidance from a financial coach? Would you go on a shopping spree and spend aimlessly? Or, would you use it to serve and enhance the lives of others? Money can empower you to accomplish many of your goals and dreams. Unfortunately, it is well documented that many lottery winners who receive large financial wind-falls usually go broke and file bankruptcy between three to five years after winning. To accomplish anything in life requires that you find your why, reason or purpose. Have you found yours?

Reason #3 – Inside or Outside the Box? - how do you think? Are you an inside of the box thinker who settles for the status quo? Someone who follows the traditional paths in life. They graduate with a post-high school formal education in their chosen field of academia. They are active income earners, working for their money on a 9 to 5 job, working the 40-40-40 plan consisting of working 40 hours per week, for 40 years of their life, living off 40% of their income during retirement. They have a company-sponsored retirement plan (457 or 401K, pension plan) and maybe some personal savings. They have enormous debt due to high credit card usage. And this group is your stereotypical investor in stocks, bonds and mutual funds as their wealth building strategy.

Or, are you an outside of the box thinker or don't see the box at all? They use the glass ceiling to see beyond their current situation. For them, there are no limits. They are risk-takers. They become entrepreneur's and start traditional brick and mortar or a home-based business while putting in long hours, day in and day out.

They are your non-status quo or alternative investors such as private equity, real estate, and cryptocurrency. They learned how to make their money work for them, rather than work for their money using passive residual streams of income! They can create massive wealth using products and or services, create jobs while contributing to the economic engine of the local and or global economy. This group of people understands that without risk (and sometimes failure) there can be no reward! This group is willing to do things that others won't so they can live like others don't! Are you willing to do what it takes to live a phenomenal life of purpose?

Reason #4 - Stuck - some people are stuck in place. For their own individual reasons, which I do not pass judgment, they have given up. They experience low self-esteem and self-worth. They are not interested in continuing self-education for self-improvement. They are frustrated and feeling overwhelmed. They feel inadequate and withdrawn from mainstream social outings and affairs. They experience helplessness and sorrow from being unfulfilled as compared to others.

Most importantly, they do not have a heart's burning desire to change and succeed. Stuck people are not open to being mentored or coached by successful people who blazed the trail before them. They don't have a Why [reason or purpose – goal or dream]. They have no vision for change, transformation or success.

Business start-up is out of the question, working a regular job is a no-no, and wealth creation is off the radar. Pulling themselves up by their own bootstraps, and changing their current situation is not on their agenda. You cannot (no matter how hard you persist) get this group to try. They have little or no faith in things unseen with the natural eye. They have no connection with the Universal-spiritual energy that surrounds their personal space here on earth. They move from day to day aimlessly, without solid plans.

They have "Stinkin Thinkin." They are pessimistic in thought, always thinking of the things that are not manifesting within their life. Instead of being optimistic and always thinking of things that will manifest within their life. They just stand in the batter's box of life, never swinging, never hitting, while watching every single pitch (opportunity) pass them by. Are you stuck? If yes, why? What are you going to do about it?

Reason #5 – Mediocre or Wealth Mindset – A Paradigm Shift - the mediocre mind is incapable of understanding the man or woman (great spirits) who refuses to bow down blindly to conventional prejudices and chooses instead to express his or her own opinions courageously and honestly.

> *"Great spirits have always encountered violent opposition from mediocre minds."*
> *-Albert Einstein*

As we all know, education is one critical path to success. Whether it is traditional education, personal development, self-improvement education, or learning from coaches and mentors, acquiring knowledge is an essential key to success. The use of knowledge is the real power.

You can stay enrolled in the University of Hard Knocks, or you can graduate with your Ph.D. from the University of Lifeology. When you learn more, chances are you will earn more! You can be streetwise or book smart or both, but if you don't put that wisdom and knowledge to good use, like Bill Gates said, "it's your mistake if you die poor."

> *"There are only seven days in a week and someday is not one of them."*
> *-Dr. Shaquille O'Neal*

It is a known fact that several millionaires and billionaires (great spirits) did not graduate from college. In other words, they discovered their moment of clarity and used their heart's burning desires and were still able to acquire vast fortunes. What are the underlying key factors that enable winners to see clearly down the road of success, when others (mediocre minds) fail to do so?

Winners don't wait for someday to come; they take action everyday! They develop the conviction to follow their heart's burning desire, despite what anyone says. They courageously march to the beat of their own drum! Remember, winners, don't believe in someday, there is only today!

Once clarity begins, a strange thing happens. You start to lose some friends and family members, but you gain another set of like-minded, supportive people in your life. It's ok to agree to disagree, especially when the goal or dream is not the same for everyone sitting at the table. When everyone's plate is full of the same vision and heart's burning desire, the group sitting at the table is now magically transformed into being— all for one, and one for all!

William Shakespeare said, "Nothing is neither good nor bad, but thinking makes it so."

You must experience a paradigm shift from a mediocre mindset to a wealth mindset to *"Find Your Moment of Clarity."* Once you have clarity you will have found your purpose and become empowered to change your life. There will be no limits to living the phenomenal life you deserve.

Now, continue on with the next transformational chapter titled Awaken To Your Soul by Elyse.

Thank You Robbie

CHAPTER 6

AWAKEN TO YOUR SOUL

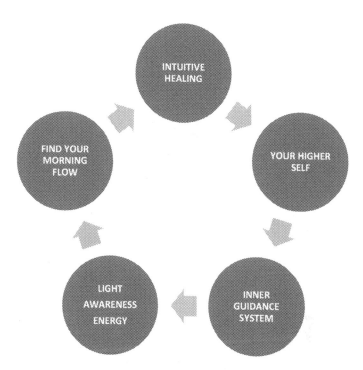

Allow me, to introduce you, to my good friend, Elyse Falzone
By Elyse Falzone

I t's pretty easy to get stuck in a rut and live your life on replay or repeat each day. Trust me. I have been there and done that before. BORING. Not only is it boring, but this monotone energy and 'going through the motions' way of living can create a low vibration and lack of desire. It can also create an illusion of unworthiness and lack of self-esteem. Many times, it takes a big smack in the face to see the way we have been living. It may be a car accident, break up from a beloved relationship, getting laid off from a job, an illness or something of the sorts. For me, it was melanoma skin cancer.

Ever since I was a kid, I knew there was something leading me, guiding me and whispering the ways of the world to me. I could sense things and feel things that could not be explained. God was showing me the Universe and instilling confidence in my intuition and Higher Self... I just didn't know it yet. In my youth, I wasn't ready for all of it, so I asked it to be halted and be revealed again when I was ready, and it was time. Ever since, my life has been a journey of rediscovering my Truth, rediscovering my heart and a reconnecting to my Higher Self (inner guidance system).

I'd like to make a request. Let THIS be your wake-up call. Don't wait for the tragedy. Don't wait for melanoma skin cancer. This can be it. Your Higher Self has had an invitation awaiting your acceptance for a long time. Now is the time to say 'YES.'

What are you saying YES to? By accepting this invitation to your soul, you are saying YES to your talents and gifts. You are saying YES to taking chances and being unapologetically YOU. You are saying YES to laughing lots and living carefree. It can seem a bit scary or overwhelming to take this leap. It can be labeled as 'unknown' territory. You may not always know the answers or what's coming next. It's ok. You'll begin to live this adventure with hope, faith, and trust.

One way to get started or take the next step on this journey is to begin to change your thinking and shift your habits. One thing that made a massive difference for me was waking up with purpose each and every day. Below I have mapped out how you can wake up feeling alive, joyful and start your day by celebrating you.

Wake with Joy: 5 Steps to Create Your Morning Flow

1. Decide you are ready and WILLING to make a change.
2. Create your personal flow. Choose 3-5 actions to formulate your flow.
   - Play your favorite song as your alarm
   - Take 3 deep breaths
   - Meditate (2 min – 20 min)
   - Say a prayer
   - Do jumping jacks
   - Look in the mirror and say I AM statements (I AM Beautiful. I AM Worthy. I AM Creative).
   - Journal (Spend 5-10 min writing)
   - Go outside in nature
   - Eat a healthy breakfast
   - Write your daily goals
   - Make a gratitude list
   - Light some candles
   - Smile
   - Create your own ritual or idea
3. Write your 3-5 actions on a sheet of paper or sticky note so you can see it and follow it each morning.
4. Give your new flow a try! (If it feels good, keep it. If it doesn't, then shift and retry it).
5. Make your new flow a habit. (Commit to at least 40 days).

When I did the exercise above and began to wake up with passion, purpose, and joy, it started to spill over into all areas of my life, in the best way possible. I began to see my worth. I began to witness the beauty of life around me. I began to hear those gentle whispers of my soul. I began to feel the rush of exhilaration as I went about my day. I began to remember my Truth. My inner child came alive again. She reminded me to dance, sing and play. Through these daily discoveries and taking the time to listen to my inner guidance, I have created a business and life I love. It's now my mission to support others in awakening to their soul's true purpose. It's time to leave a legacy.

Now it's your turn. Remember, YOU are the only you. You are unique, and your gifts are needed on this planet. If you were to close your eyes right now and ask yourself, "What is it that I truly desire?" I'll bet your heart knows the answer. You may be afraid to speak what is revealed, but it is there. If it's hard to come up with the answer, keep asking. You may have just buried your Truth so deep and so many times, that it may take a moment to surface.

Once you are ready to honor that answer, it's all about taking steps to awaken it. This is the part I love! I have gotten to witness so many people saying YES to their dreams and soul's calling. What is yours? Is it to open a bakery, start a non-profit, design sets for musicals, open a yoga studio, travel the world or become a life coach or spiritual teacher? You have everything inside of you already. You are beautiful. You are powerful. You are brilliant. Own it. Be it. Inspire others to do the same. Your legacy awaits you.

Thank You Elyse

CHAPTER 7

TAKE A STROLL THROUGH YOUR MIND

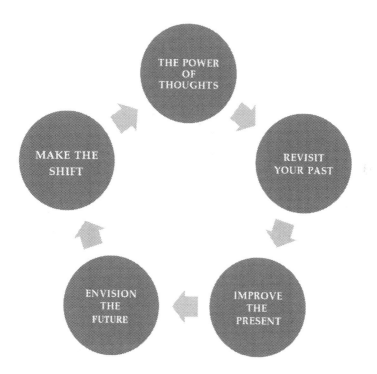

By Michael Bart Mathews

W e can develop a positive mental attitude by shifting our conscious thought toward transformation and success. We can learn how to use our invisible antenna and piggyback onto our vibrational superhighway, by tapping into our invisible communication command center. Once onboard, we can raise our frequency level and dive deep into our subconscious mind. This illuminating glow will help generate more positive light, awareness, opportunity, and success, on our journey while we are *"Finding Our Moment of Clarity."*

Like Dorothy, in the Wizard of Oz, and ET, they both developed the positive mental attitude that they would make it back home in spite of every challenge.

We are at our best when the synchronicity of our conscious mind (while we are awake) and our subconscious mind (while we are both awake & sleep) are both firing on all cylinders. We are in that positive, mental creative energy zone filled with the highest level of Universal power at our disposal. Ideas seem to appear out of thin air, as if you rubbed on a magic lamp and your genie named "Creativity" appeared.

Take a quiet stroll through your mind, using your internal guidance system and mentally time travel back. Revisit past decisions you made after you engage in deep thought or meditation. Do you see your "stinkin thinkin," your fears and other emotional baggage blockers that held you back?

Now, think about those decisions that became your change agents for achievement. Those thought leadership decisions that enabled you to overcome whatever obstacles or adversities that blocked you from change and success from the start. Now shift your thoughts toward the countless achievements and successes that you experienced in life. Like the strength and courage that Elyse showed in her story in Chapter 6 above. How did you, as an ordinary person, attract and manifest extraordinary change and accomplishments?

The answer is; even if you did not know this to be true, you made the decision to change how you were thinking, acting and feeling about the situation.

"F.E.A.R. can either represent:
Forget Everything And Run
or
Face Everything And Rise."
- James Dentley

When babies are small, they have a fear of falling and the fear of loud noises. Concerning anything else, they are the most inquisitive little people around. As babies grow older, the more they learn, the more fearful they become of certain realities, new experiences, and challenges. Now that full grown adult who has developed negative thoughts and the fear of failure, in many cases never will reach his or her full potential. They allowed the fear or False Evidence Appearing Real to stymie their success. FEAR can look different for different people.

What fears from your own negative experiences or self-inflicted, self-imposed thoughts are holding you back from making a positive change? What negative thoughts and emotional baggage blockers can you change in your mindset that will help you look at the glass as being half full of change and opportunity, and not half empty with self-defeat from your own thoughts? Remember to set and reset the bar of your positive thoughts high enough so you can eat the elephant of transformation change, and success, one bite at a time!

Are you starving hungry for change because of your positive thoughts? Do you possess the unwavering faith, fully believing that you can do it? Are you discovering your heart's burning desire deep down within your soul? Are you persistent with your actions toward achievement? Are you mastering how to use your imagination (visualizing the end result) and daring to dream big dreams? Then the power of your positive thoughts can assist you in *"Finding Your Moment of Clarity."* This might sound like double talk, but change is not change until you change!

> *"There is nothing wrong with change, as long as it's in the right direction."*
> -Winston Churchill

You must look in the mirror and hold that person who is staring back at you accountable for how you think, feel and act. Your self-help, personal development, self-actualization, and ongoing never-ending positive change for success is your responsibility and yours alone. Not your parents, not your brother, not your sister, not your neighbor, and not your friend. You are responsible for your health, personal and financial growth, service to others, success, love, light, joy, and happiness!

Not even your spouse or significant other is responsible for your success! True enough, they can be a crucial factor and play a vital supportive role in your ongoing quest for success. They will be your number one cheerleader; they will be a sounding board to bounce your ideas off when need be. They will be a helping hand and a listening ear when you need to talk. They can be a think tank or mastermind group member willing to agree and disagree with you along your journey. With all this positive support, if you don't take action toward achievement, you will become a wondering generality or a wasted talent, not being seen at all. The world will see you in one of three ways. 1. A great memory. 2. A terrible reminder. 3. A wasted talent, not seeing you at all.

Stop for a moment, look around at everything that you see. This entire world that we live in, besides nature, was made by the inner thoughts from men and women who had creative ideas, and developed their heart's burning desire for change and success. They worked tirelessly around the clock turning that idea into a tangible reality in the form of a product or service.

Because of our ability to use our brain and think things into existence, beginning with an idea from thought, having singleness of purpose, taking the right action, and never quitting until accomplishment, the world has benefited from the constant change. Because of men and women all around the globe using creative ideas from thought, new innovative and exciting inventions, products and services have always sprung up from one generation to the next generation.

Here are a few *"Finding Your Moment of Clarity"* examples:

The light bulb invented by Thomas Edison in (1879). The Henry Ford Company founded in (1901). Madam C. J. Walker (hair care products), first recorded Black Millionaire (early 1900's). Warren Buffet began buying stock in Berkshire Hathaway (1962) and purchased Berkshire Hathaway (1965). Apollo eleven, first space flight to land humans on the moon (1969). Martin Cooper invented the first handheld cellular mobile phone (1973). Bill Gates & Paul Allen founded Microsoft in (1975). Steve Jobs and Steve Wozniak invented Apple Computer (1976). Robert Johnson founded "BET" Black Entertain Television (1980). The Oprah Winfrey Show (1986). Larry Page founded Google (1996).

Reid Hoffman founded LinkedIn (2002). Niklas Zennstrom and Janus Friss founded Skype (2003). Elon Musk co-founded Tesla (2003). Mark Zuckerberg co-founded Facebook (2004). Jack Dorsey, Evan Williams, Biz Stone, and Noah Glass introduced the full public version of Twitter (2006). Evan Sharp and Paul Sciarra launched Pinterest (2009). Kevin Systrom and Mike Krieger launched Instagram (2010). Evan Spiegel founded Snapchat (2011), and The Oprah Winfrey Network-OWN founded (2011).

Let's not forget about the millions upon millions of home-based business start-ups all around the world. The early historical mom and pop businesses that paved the way for others.

They all are perfect examples that thoughts do become things! If they can do it, then why not you? How many thoughts come to mind that you never act upon? Your idea, goal, dream or vision could be the world's next big transformational breakthrough product or service. Your idea can become the next global game change agent!

The Universe which we live in is vast in size and goes on until infinity and beyond. The planets in the solar system, the sun, the earth, the moon, and the stars were not made by man. A Universal, spiritual, energy source, with infinite intelligence far surpassing the thought of mankind, I believe is present. Each one of us has the ability to tap into this abundant source of energy and power when we can recognize its existence.

Depending on your Universal beliefs, based on the thoughts within your mind, all things are possible to those who believe! You can achieve success, become a leader, build up self-confidence, and enhance your power within. The fact that you can accomplish anything that you can believe means, first you must think it, then you must believe it, and then you must take action in order to transform the desired outcome for yourself!

No one has succeeded in life without experiencing highs and lows, up and downs, failures or setbacks. When you need to pull yourself up by your bootstraps, go back to the specific character-building point of reference within the pages of this book that initially inspired and motivated you. Read and reread that particular section until you are able to put into practice whatever changes that your heart desires.

That person who you see in the mirror of life is depending on you to find your heart's burning desire for change and success! My goal, as well as every special guest contributing author, is to assist you in finding your heart's burning desire by helping you to wake up that sleeping giant from within your mind, body, spirit, and soul.

The awesome secret sauce to success is you! First, you must think it. Next, you must believe it, and only then can you achieve it! If you want it bad enough, your persistence (taking action) toward change or success must outweigh or supersede the fear of failure. The only way you can be persistent is that you take action (develop success habits) over and over again. You must understand how important it is to become a meaningful specific, having your laser beam focused on your goal. Then and only then, will you no longer be a wandering generality.

You will have clarity in your mission once you decide what it is that you really want to do in life? Once you can answer that question from serious thought-provoking meditation, think tank or mastermind sessions, and coaching, only then can the Universe help you find a way to make it happen.

Why were the new seven wonders of the world built? The New Seven Wonders of the World, selected in 2007 are; the ancient Mayan city of Chichen Itza in Mexico, Christ the Redeemer statue in Rio de Janeiro-Brazil, Great Wall of China, Machu Picchu the Inca ruins in Peru, Taj Mahal in India, Petra in Jordan and the Colosseum in Rome Italy. You can add the Great Barrier Reef in Australia, the Grand Canyon & Niagara Falls-United States, and the Great Egyptian Pyramids at Giza, not far from Cairo.

I make mention of the Seven Wonders of the World because people all around the world have big ideas from positive mental thought with accomplishment while visioning the end in mind. To showcase another undeniable fact that someone first had an idea from thought, they believed they could build it and lastly, they took action until they achieved it. Again, that is the awesome secret sauce for change and success.

Just like then, just like now, the same philosophy holds true from the wheel to the rocket ship, from the windup telephone to the modern day, ever-changing, handheld smartphones. The missing link for success for many people is that they do not think they can succeed, and they do not possess a heart filled with a burning desire for change or success. One must have singleness of purpose for accomplishment that comes from that burning desire within.

Examine yourself, somewhere deep down within your core soul, that sleeping giant called "your hearts burning desire" is ever-present. You have the ability to be your own magic genie in the bottle. You can grant yourself as many wishes (ideas, goals & dreams) as your heart desires.

In the ancient story of Aladdin, he possessed a magic lamp. Whenever he rubbed the magic lamp, a powerful genie would appear and grant his every wish, and desires.

Today, I refer to the brain (thoughts) as being the magic genie inside of our heads. To summon our magic genie (thoughts) we must first be consciously aware and awake to it's never ending powers. The difference between the story of Aladdin's magic lamp and man's use of the brain is that we are the possessor of our own never-ending magic genie called thought. We don't have to physically rub our brains, but we must think, then take action, in order for our goals and dreams to manifest. We can summon thought anytime, anywhere, anyplace! From thought (our magic genie) comes ideas!

> "People become really quite remarkable when they start thinking that they can do things. When they believe in themselves, they have the first secret of success. "
> -Norman Vincent Peale

Success is the progressive realization of a worthy ideal or dream! It is your WHY [reason or purpose - goal or dream] that counts! How big is your dream? I remember reading that a person's dreams should be so big, that they can't be accomplished in one lifetime! That means if you aim for the moon, you will hit some stars along the way. Isn't it better to collect the dust from your shooting star, rather than stand in the shadows of a falling star?

Fear is a significant deal breaker between change, success, and failure. What do you have to lose if you fail? As long as failure doesn't defeat you, it should make you bigger, better, and stronger, as long as you don't keep making the same mistakes. Failure is simply finding out what doesn't work, until you crack the success code because you are persistent enough to find out what did work!

> Thomas Edison – "I have not failed 10,000 times. I have not failed once. I have concluded that those 10,000 ways will not work. When I have eliminated the ways that will not work, I will find the way that will work."

Ordinary people can and have accomplished extraordinary things because winners never quit, and quitters never win! The choice is yours and yours alone to make! You have become what you have been thinking about all your life. As we grow older, our thoughts continuously change, and our current everyday situation is a mirror image of how we think, feel and act in the present. Having core principal centered values, and singleness of purpose, you can accomplish your heart's burning desire.

Your past, with the help of deep thought and meditation, is a porthole or superhighway back into time. A time in which you can remember both good and bad experiences. The past is also a springboard of what the future holds, depending on what you choose-to hold steadfast within your consciousness. Hold the good times and the positive outcomes as your vessel of steel to overcome fear and to achieve more of the same. Use the bad times, negative outcomes as your vessel of encouragement, having a full understanding that you will never repeat the same mistakes because doing so is insane.

There are countless visions, ideas, goals, and dreams remaining to be accomplished by those who willingly pick up the mantel and accepts the torch that is passed on to them. The struggle is part of change and success! You are not unique in this regard! Struggling is one of many tests that we must undertake within the Universe to survive, thrive, and yes, become successful.

Take the metamorphosis process of the caterpillar, once encased within their chrysalis (the moths form a cocoon), for one of nature's examples of struggle first, reward second! The caterpillar must endure the act of struggle until it has its breakthrough moment of freedom, as it is transforming into a beautiful butterfly. With plenty of effort, and without any kind of outside help, the caterpillar will be able to fulfill its destiny of transformation. When the butterfly emerges, it is unable to fly because its wings are small and wet. After a growth and exercise cycle, the butterfly is able to take flight.

Like the struggle of the metamorphosis transformation process of the caterpillar to the beautiful butterfly, the Universe has made struggle a part of success for those who are willing to endure their own metamorphosis process toward the visions, goals, and dreams in that which they seek.

Like the caterpillar's determination, desire and persistence to reach butterfly status and live on, you must have the same focus and determination during your times of struggle. First, embrace your struggle, then keep on fighting until you experience your breakthrough moment of clarity. Imagine you are no longer the struggling caterpillar. Imagine achieving your goals, and now you have transformed yourself into the beautiful butterfly experiencing results and success in that which you seek.

I did not say transformation, change or success was going to be easy. But I will say, nothing ventured, nothing gained! Like the lines in William Shakespeare's play, Hamlet, "To be or Not to Be, that is the question." I want to make this perfectly clear, the use of any internal energy stemming from past generational events should only be channeled into positive, personal development, meaningful acts of good deeds and kindness toward all mankind, beginning with self.

Think back for a moment and once again mentally travel back in time and zero in on a very difficult time in your past. Remember the trials and tribulations that came along during that period of struggle. Now reflect back on the breakthrough events as you were *Finding Your Moment of Clarity.* You found clarity because you forged on despite those struggles. You achieved success back then, and you can achieve success while breaking through your struggles right here, right now, today.

> *"You can do anything you want, even if you are being told negative things. Stay strong and find motivation."*
> -Misty Copeland

Once that reflection that you see staring back at you in the mirror is in Universal positive harmony, only then can that person help themselves as well as others! Misty Copeland (June 30th, 2015) became the first African American performer to be appointed principal dancer with the American Ballet Theatre founded in 1937. Ballet became Misty's heart's burning desire. And you can *Find Your Moment of Clarity* as well! Do you think Misty Copeland had to overcome struggles? You can bet your last dollar, that she did. And you can too.

Read on and discover "that special something," your heart's burning desire that can enable you to succeed despite whatever struggles or obstacles you might be facing. Even when someone is constantly feeding you negative words and energy and telling you that you can't succeed! Remember; quitters never win!

The real secret to finding your heart's burning desire is locked up somewhere inside your mind. It's itching, scratching, clawing, digging, shouting, begging and hoping that you will unlock the trap door and free it from mediocrity! It wants to rise up like the Phoenix, out of the burning ashes of struggle and make new, positive wings of contributions in the ongoing journey towards self-achievement in the areas of your choosing.

Like the rebirth of the mythical Phoenix who rose from the burning ashes of struggles, you too can rise from whatever it is that is holding you back from what you want to achieve in life. Imagine getting rid of those emotional baggage blockers once and for all! It all begins with your WHY [reason or purpose-goal or dream] most importantly, your vision.

HOW BIG IS YOUR DREAM? Not having a dream is one of the reasons why a vast amount of people will never reach their full peak potential in life.

> *Earvin Magic Johnson – "If people around you aren't going anywhere. If their dreams are no bigger than hanging out on the corner, or if they're dragging you down, get rid of them. Negative people can sap your energy so fast, and they can take your dreams from you, too."*

Now that you have taken a stroll through your mind, what have you discovered about yourself? Are you now another step closer toward reaching your greatest potential and a higher level of achievement? Are you overcoming your fears and limiting beliefs? What does your vision look like now?

Are you going to be a leader, an action taker or a follower? The choice is yours! Read on to continue your journey to *"Finding Your Moment of Clarity."*

CHAPTER 8

THE ART OF MEDITATION

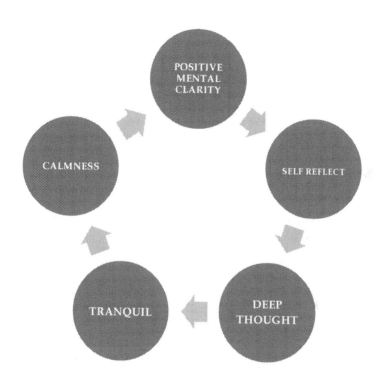

By Michael Bart Mathews

M editation can help you discover *"Finding Your Moment of Clarity"* and your power within by helping you to facilitate change in your life. Like when you are driving on the throughway or highway inside urban city limits. The minimum speed limit is 45 miles per hour. The posted speed limit is fifty-five miles per hour. Slow moving vehicles use the right lane. When you reach the open rural area, in some cases, the speed limit increases or changes to seventy miles per hour.

If the vehicle in front of you is traveling at the minimum speed of forty-five or doing the posted limit of fifty-five miles per hour, what must you do to increase your speed to the new seventy-mile per hour limit? You must take action by activating your turn signal indicating your desire to change lanes. Next, check your mirror for clarity. Finally, you must accelerate and most importantly, change lanes while maintaining a clear vision of the open road in front, behind, and on the side.

After you complete passing the slower moving vehicle, you must once again signal your intentions to change lanes, check your mirrors for clarity and proceed to change back into the right lane.

And so it is in life, you must have a clear vision of the lane you choose in life if you don't want more of the same! Think about this; *Muhammad Ali: "That if at age fifty, you still see life as you did at age twenty, then you have wasted thirty years of your life."* You must learn how to transform how you think, act, and feel today, to experience different results tomorrow! You cannot keep thinking the same thoughts, and you cannot keep doing the same things expecting a different outcome and change in your life at the same time!

Meditation is one way of helping you to draw out of your mind, new ideas from deep thoughts, from several different areas of your life. You already hold the master keys to success within your mind. Meditation can assist you in unlocking the trap door of your mental vault filled with untapped ideas.

Meditation can play a vital role in the transformation of your mind, body, and actions. You can focus in on exactly what it is that you want to change or accomplish. You can allow your mind to free flow or wander across time and space. You can develop the ability to allow your thoughts to levitate or float out of thin air or drift like the free spirit of an eagle in flight using the wind beneath its wings to glide effortlessly in the direction of its next destination. When you master how to take a stroll through your mind, you might be surprised at what you might find!

The Merriam- Webster definition for "Meditate" is as follows:

1. To engage in contemplation or reflection.
2. To engage in mental exercise to reach a heightened level of spiritual awareness.
3. To focus on one's thoughts: reflect on or ponder over.
4. To plan a project in your mind.

After you put into practice and master steps one through four listed above, step number five, the most critical factor of all is; you must without fail, physically transfer your thoughts from your mind into reality! In written form, on paper, with a date of accomplishment, followed by an action plan for success. Remember: when you fail to plan, you plan to fail!

This will assist you in becoming a meaningful specific (having and seeing a clear vision) unlike the wandering generality (no clear focus or vision) having no thought-provoking plan of action or date of accomplishment for achievement. Meditation is a mental based action exercise. Sooner or later you must take physical action toward change and accomplishment.

Do you want to feel more positive about achieving your goals, hopes, visions, and dreams? Do you want to have better personal relationships with your spouse, family, friends, and co-workers? Do you want a better sense of personal fulfillment? Do you want to be happier? If you answered yes to any one of these questions, then you are an excellent candidate for practicing the Art of Meditation.

The Art of Meditation has been practiced by civilizations for thousands of years dating back to ancient times. It is suggested, that during the primitive hunter-gatherer period in history, that society may have discovered meditation (altered states of consciousness) while staring at the flickering flames while sitting around the burning fire, cooking or trying to stay warm.

Moving forward in history, Buddha, one of Asia's most notable meditation teachers, is famous for his methods and usage of mindfulness practices. His world-famous methods have been practiced by millions of people from several different generations, including today.

The power of thought (meditation) being used for personal growth/self-improvement within the mind of the practitioner (you) and me from Buddha:

> "The mind is everything, what you think you become."
>
> -Buddha

> ➤ "We are shaped by our thoughts; we become what we think. When the mind is pure, joy follows like a shadow that never leaves."
> ➤ "To be idle is a short road to death, and to be diligent is a way of life; foolish people are idle, wise people are diligent."
> ➤ "We are what we think. All that we are arises with our thoughts. With our thoughts, we make the world."

Marcus Aurelius, the Philosopher, was the Emperor of Rome. He wrote page after page of meditations from his personal thoughts as a source for his own guidance and self-improvement. He titled his literary writings; *To Myself,* because he depended heavily on his own philosophy and spirituality of thought. You and I have the same ability as did Marcus Aurelius! The title was later changed to *Meditations.*

Listed below are some quotes by Marcus Aurelius and his own practical understanding of the power of thought (meditation) being used for self-improvement/personal growth within his own mind, as well as in the mind of the practitioner (you and me):

> "The happiness of your life depends upon the quality of your thoughts."
>
> -Marcus Aurelius

> ➤ *"You have the power over your mind – not outside events. Realize this, and you will find strength."*
> ➤ *"Our life is what our thoughts make it."*
> ➤ *"A man's worth is no greater than his ambitions."*
> ➤ *"Observe constantly that all things take place by change and accustom thyself to consider that the nature of the Universe loves nothing so much as to change things which are, and to make new things like them."*

Buddha and Marcus Aurelius both understood mindfulness, self-actualization and the power of personal development and self-improvement for change that comes from taking control of one's thoughts. They (you have the same ability) transformed their everyday thoughts into positive affirmations. Still today, the secret to success in any area of your life comes from the positive power of your own thoughts. How you think, act and feel are major components for positive change and success for all who seeks her wisdom!

Phil Jackson has been called "The Zen Master." He is one of the most successful and winningest NBA coaches of all time. He has eleven NBA championships to his credit. Phil Jackson has used the *Art of Meditation – Zen Buddhism* philosophy of mindfulness to help build mental strength among his players (Chicago Bulls & L.A. Lakers) during their professional championship basketball playing days.

Coach Jackson has often shared his beliefs in the positive aspects that one can gain from practicing the *Art of Meditation*. Phil Jackson also recommended books for his players to read (we will discuss the Five-Hour Rule in Chapter 24) in the comfort and privacy of their downtime. His goal was to assist his players on how to learn how to stay cool, calm and collective on the basketball court when under pressure during intense games.

It is evident that Phil Jackson is a very successful person, both on and off the basketball court. His players were able to experience the highest level of basketball success, over and over and over under his leadership. What role would you say that the *Art of Meditation* played in winning those championships? What did each individual player discover within themselves that allowed them to achieve team success using techniques from the *Art of Meditation – The Zen Buddhism* philosophy of mindfulness? Was it a critical pivotal factor to their team's success?

Phil Jackson believed that "Spirituality is about the ability to incorporate other beings into your plans, in what you're doing, or saying, in your day – to – day job. It's keeping in mind, 'My actions create actions that other people have to deal with. And my best nature elevates their nature."

Here are several tips to assist you with the *Art of Meditation*, regardless if you decide to use music or not. Keep in mind that different people use different methods. There is no right or wrong approach. Decide which methods work best for you and what does not work. Develop your own strategy or system and follow that plan until you obtain the desired results that you seek. Or seek a certified, experienced Meditation Coach to teach and guide you through the *Art of Meditation*.

- Choose a time that is convenient and works for you (early morning or late at night works for me). You can meditate almost anywhere once you are in sync with your internal guidance system and have better control over your thoughts.

> *"To make the right choices in life, you have to get in touch with your soul. To do this, you need to experience solitude, which most people are afraid of, because in the silence you hear the truth and know the solutions."*
> *-Deepak Chopra*

- Choose how long you will meditate (I have a minimum set time 10 to 30 minutes, but I fully relax and go with the flow) depending on time constraints.

- Choose a comfortable, quiet place of solitude, where you will be alone that generates free flowing high energy (I like sitting at the kitchen table or in my living room chair).

- Sit upright and make sure you are comfortable. Some people lay in bed just before sleeping and just after awakening. Others use their couch. (I do this, depending on my energy flow). Make sure you are as relaxed as can be.

- Keep a soft, warm, gentle smile on your face. Think of a happy moment, then hold that smile for a while, I sometimes use Laughter Yoga to make myself laugh (see contributing author Amy Sayama in Chapter 10). The one thing that we all desire, or should desire is to be happy, healthy and have peace of mind if nothing else.

- Now close your eyes and begin your session of meditation using your own mental thoughts. You can direct or shift your thoughts in the direction of your choice, or you can go with the free flow of thought. Allow the Universe to plant her seeds within your mind in the present, or across time and space from yesteryear while mentally time traveling back into the past. Imagine using the application of clairvoyant practice (one who sees clearly) as you explore your future (vision). Don't worry about the time! Relax, stay free-spirited and allow your ideas from thought to flow.

- When coming to the end of your meditation sessions, slowly open your eyes and transition from out of the darkness back into the light. Take your time getting back on your feet. The transfer of energy through meditation back into the present state of reality has different effects on different people. I've witnessed people become unbalanced or dizzy because of a lack of experience. This seldom happens, nevertheless, take the necessary precautions.

Reflect back on what you thought about and most importantly, how you felt about it. This is when new ideas come to light with little effort. Write down that a-ha moment from any sudden insights you discover. Sometimes you will draw a blank on new ideas, and other times you will discover the answers to some of the most complex issues that you might be facing. Thus, using your thoughts from meditation, you have conjured up new ideas.

Thoughts that are not written down are like young, inexperienced migrating birds in flight, they will fly out of your mind and may be lost forever. Only allow positive thoughts to nest in your mind. Think of your mind as being an eagle's nest of positive eggs filled with ideas! You can build your positive mental nest one thought at a time, like the eagle build's it's nest one straw at a time. Your mind is like a pulling magnet; it attracts conditions that are in direct correlation with your thoughts from either positive or negative entries.

This will also give you a written record of what and when you had the transformation, and from which meditation session it occurred. When you think positive thoughts, they will usually have good, uplifting positive emotional feelings. When you think negative thoughts, they will usually have uncomfortable or negative emotional feelings and outcomes. Learn how to get in the vortex and channel your positive mental thoughts, feelings, actions, and emotions.

During your meditative state of thought, your inner guidance system; which is equivalent to the GPS-Global Positioning Satellite used for directional navigation, kicks in. Your inner mind, your internal guidance system of thought becomes your directional MapQuest for rational thought. You are responsible for programming your journey as well as navigating the many different paths and directions that are available. The same way you talk or type your destination in Google Maps, or MapQuest and you activate the trip start button, you have the same ability to mind-map yourself and chart out your life's destiny. Google Maps and MapQuest will re-route your trip when you veer off course. As with you, you have the same mind-mapping ability to re-chart your course of thought toward your desired destination in life.

We often go through life without taking a full, honest, ongoing examination of ourselves and our current situation in life. We play the blame game for why we are not where we think we should be. We hardly ever take an honest self-assessment or mental snapshot of what we can do to help ourselves to discover the real energy and power within.

The ability of the mind being able to think positive, meaningful thoughts is the governing factor of our everyday lives. We make decisions that will affect our lives until the day we depart from this earth.

Once you discover that you ended up where you are in life today because of the sum total of your thoughts, actions or lack of action, either positive or negative, your journey will never be the same. Instead of allowing someone else to have the opportunity to say something like, "I knew you couldn't do it." Why not develop a positive mental attitude using mind-mapping & thought leadership? As long as you take the necessary action for success, and don't quit until you succeed, then the nay-sayers will say, "how did you do it, or you were lucky?"

How we think (positive thoughts), act (ongoing actions) and feel (our magnetic emotions) will always be the game changer that separates the winners from the losers. Always begin with the end in mind, and don't stop until you cross the finish line!

The Art of Meditation can help you build a positive mental attitude against fear and procrastination, which is the assassination of success. You really only fail when you give up and stop trying! Remember; procrastination is the assassination of success! If you are looking for a new belief system, give the Art of Meditation and mind-mapping your own mind some serious thought.

Remember that practicing the *Art of Meditation* has a high probability of yielding many different results for different people. You are not in competition with any other person. The *Art of Meditation* is another way for you to get in touch with your internal mind. By sharpening up your inner guidance system, you will be on your journey to *"Finding Your Moment of Clarity."*

CHAPTER 9

ALL ABOUT MINDSET

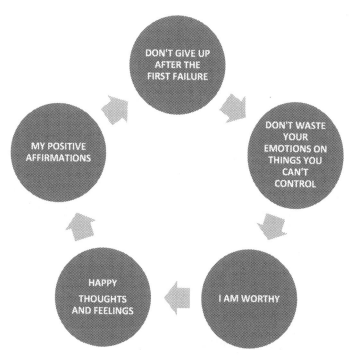

Allow me, to introduce you, to my friend, Karel Vermeulen
By Karel Vermeulen

M y mind is always busy—always thinking ahead, with so many things at the same time, it seems like I'm talking to myself. If someone had to record my thoughts, they would think I lost the plot and needed to be admitted to a psychiatric institution.

To the outside world, I seem like a positive person who is completely in control. This was not always the case. You see, I will be the first to admit that, even today, I still struggle with signs of depression, loneliness, destructive thoughts, anger, and even doubts in myself. Yes, despite my success. One thing I pride myself on is that when I get these thoughts and feelings, I'll ponder over them for a day or two, feel sorry for myself, and then, miraculously, I'll get myself out of it! This is an effective coping mechanism I've learned over the years.

How do I do that? I utilize the power of my mind by talking positively to myself. Let me give you an example:

When I am in a state of depression, I will, at some point, begin telling myself the following: "Karel, this is not worth it. I am much better than this. This is not going to win the battle to defeat me. I must pick myself up–no one is going to do this for me. This state I am in is not doing anybody any good. Put on your big boy pants. I must earn a living, and if I do not pick myself up and get out of this situation, I will not have money to pay my debts and enjoy a good living!"

You see, it's a positive method of self-talk, and I must say, it's amazing when you start doing this. How your mind begins to believe it, and how the situation changes. We all have our struggles and down days. It is all about what we are doing with those days. Are you lying in self-pity all the time, or are you going to pick yourself up, wipe away your tears, and become a stronger, better person and learn from it?

I am a strong self-motivator. I had to learn that from a very young age; I had no one who believed in me or encouraged me to be successful. I believe that motivation does not come from outside forces or circumstances alone. How many times have you been to a motivational speaker, felt inspired to go and change your situation or world, and a few days later, you're still where you were before you went to the event?

It all starts between your ears. Your belief system. What do you believe to be true about yourself? You can only act out what you believe. As the saying goes: Whatever you believe to be true in a certain situation–that is true to you.

Your beliefs provide your motivation, and together with your motivation, hard, smart work, and discipline (habits), you will get your desired results. Don't get me wrong. You can't simply believe and expect that magic will happen. You need to be true to yourself, accept where you are, and begin to act accordingly. No actions–no results!

Have you heard the saying that, "your attitude determines your altitude?" I'm sure you have. "Attitude drives actions. Actions drive results. Results drive lifestyles." This quote is from American business philosopher, Jim Rohn.[1]

Our minds are extremely powerful. Everything starts with a thought planted as a seed. It is up to you to water that seed, so that it grows into a plant, by being mindful about that thought and acting accordingly. The choice is up to you whether you want to learn how to use more of your mind power or not.

My life completely turned around 360 degrees for the better in 2011, when I attended a mind power seminar. I immediately started implementing some of the very basic principles. I was blown away to realize what a huge influence my mind had on my actions and my belief system.

I did, however, walk out of that seminar, because at that specific moment in time, the way the seminar was conducted was not what I needed. My mindset and emotions were not in line to accept the truth about what they were teaching. Although I walked out, this extremely powerful affirmation stuck in my mind:

---

1   America's Business Philosopher, www.jimrohn.com

*"My thoughts, my words, and my actions
are powerful forces of attraction."* [2]

It was a shock to my system when I had to admit to myself that I was the reason I was not successful. That money was not coming into my life as I thought it would. That I was the reason why so many negative things were happening in my life, all because of my programmed negative thinking and the negative words I spoke about myself.

Subconsciously, I programmed my mind to attract all these bad and negative results in my life. Wow, what a shocker and eye-opener it was. So, what did I do? I started to write down some positive affirmations that I would say out loud to myself in my flat daily. Even when I did not believe them, I said them to myself, always expressing positivity, as if they were already true. It was not easy, I must admit, but the more I did it, the easier it became for me to believe. I even recorded it on my phone so I could listen to it while walking on the beach and while falling asleep.

One of the most important truths I learned was "that I am worthy enough" to have whatever my heart desired and the universe wants to give me. The important aspect here is not to look for a reason why you are worthy enough. When you do that, you'll find a limited belief in your mind, and you'll automatically want to find a reason why you're not worthy enough. The fact that I am alive today is reason enough to make me worthy to have all that my heart desires and have all my dreams come true.

A comfort zone is never a good place or mental state to find yourself in. There is no growth in a comfort zone. It is a zone of safety of complacency, of comfort and certainly no financial growth. The following are some characteristics of being in a comfort zone:

---

2   Mind Power into the 21st Century, John Kehoe

- A dull life
- Fear
- Procrastination
- Just getting by
- Play it safe
- Regret
- Being like everyone else
- Surviving
- Settling for less
- Being part of 98% of the population

The important question you must ask yourself is whether you want to be like the 98% of the population or do you want to be like the few 2% who are in control of their mindset while experiencing the following:

- Confidence
- Happiness
- Fulfillment
- Excitement
- Abundance
- Living without limits
- Going after their dreams
- Embracing the unknown
- Liking change
- Act despite fear
- Joy

Let me give you some examples to help you create your own worthy and positive affirmations:

I AM WORTHY

- I am worthy to have all my dreams come true
- I am worthy to be loved and to love
- I am worthy to be successful in everything I do
- I am worthy to wear beautiful clothes
- I am worthy to have my own house

> ➤ I am worthy to have all my financial needs met
> ➤ I am worthy to drive an expensive car
> ➤ I am worthy to have beautiful furniture
> ➤ I am worthy to be happy
> ➤ I am worthy to go on regular getaways and vacations

MY POSITIVE AFFIRMATIONS

> ➤ I am a highly successful strategic business entrepreneur
> ➤ I am self-motivated
> ➤ I am a great product developer
> ➤ I am a self-starter
> ➤ I am friendly and generous
> ➤ I am financially free and deserve to earn $___amount per month. (You decide what amount of money you want to earn per month and add it in.)
> ➤ I am tenacious
> ➤ I am prosperous in everything I do
> ➤ I am responsible for my own success
> ➤ I am healthy, fit, lean, and masculine
> ➤ I am a smart and hard worker
> ➤ I am a great listener
> ➤ I am a passionate and great inspirational speaker
> ➤ I am happy
> ➤ I am calm, focused, determined, and I achieve my goals

You see what I'm doing here? Now you do the same. Start right now and write your own "Worthy and Positive Affirmation List." Then repeat it every single day until it becomes part of you.

I learned to love to work out in the gym or go for a run in the forest. Many times, I did not feel like working out, but once I started and finished, I felt refreshed and energized. In the beginning, it was not easy, but as I persisted, it became second nature. I had to force myself many times just to get out of bed. My morning ritual became a habit, and now it is very easy for me to get myself to do some sort of physical activity. Now I reap the reward of a healthy and fit body.

Just like our muscles need to be trained on a regular basis, you must train your mind regularly to stay mentally fit and strong. You can accomplish anything that you set your mind to. You can be whoever you want to be. Oprah, Richard Branson, Ray Croc (McDonald's) and many more highly successful individuals often were up against high odds and with determination became a success. Some of these individuals became a success later in life, but they never gave up, and their passion and actions turned them into a major successful figure. If it can happen to them, it can happen to you. They defied the odds and made it happen. If they can do it, so can you.

What you require is a strong belief that you deserve it as much as anyone else. You will be like a magnet. You will begin to attract the right opportunities and people who can get you there. Some will succeed faster than others, and some will succeed much easier than others, but we all have the chance to succeed no matter what circumstances we face.

12 TIPS ON BUILDING MENTAL TOUGHNESS

1. Don't fear alone time.
2. Don't dwell on the past.
3. Don't feel the world owes you.
4. Don't expect immediate results.
5. Don't waste time feeling sorry for yourself.
6. Don't worry about pleasing everyone.
7. Don't waste energy on things you can't control.
8. Don't let others influence your emotions.
9. Don't resent other people's success.
10. Don't shy away from responsibilities.
11. Don't give up after the first failure.
12. Don't fear taking calculated risks.

How you change is how you succeed. How can you expect to have better or different results if you repeatedly do the same things, thinking you will have a better outcome? Get out of your comfort zone, challenge yourself, and you will be amazed to see and experience positive results.

I love this statement from Kerwin Rae: "In order for you to hit that next level for you to grow in your business, the fact remains that you must be willing to grow. And growth equals discomfort."[3]

We need to learn to be comfortable by being uncomfortable. I know this is not a good place to be, but believe me, it is worth it. Again, what is your mindset?

Learn to love discomfort. Embrace it as your friend. We need to change and adjust our thinking. Not everything we think is bad is bad for us. It is there to serve us, to guide us, and to enlighten us to grow. Discomfort in business will not kill you. But it will make you a whole lot stronger. Discomfort is good!

LESSONS LEARNED

➢ Never underestimate the power of your mind
➢ Practice daily positive affirmations
➢ It's okay to feel down or have a bad day. Pick yourself up
➢ You are your greatest motivator
➢ Learn to be comfortable by being uncomfortable

Thank You Karel

---

3   Kerwin Rae, www.kerwinrae.com

THE ART OF LAUGHTER YOGA

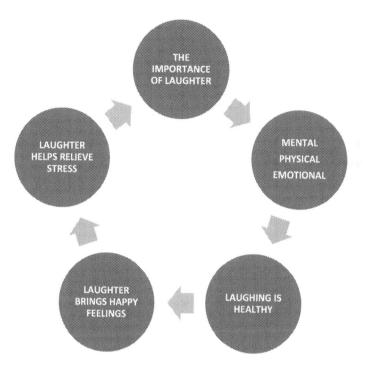

Allow me, to introduce you, to my good friend, Amy Sayama
By Amy Sayama

MIND AND BODY IN PERFECT HEALTH

L iving in an urban society, ordinary everyday task matters. Our tasks can get out of alignment, and out of optimal health. The lessons in Deepak Chopra's book titled: *Perfect Health* address the whole body and mind approach to the daily challenges and imbalances. According to Amazon, "It is a guide to harnessing the healing power of the mind." The book described how breakthroughs in physics and medicine were underscoring the validity of a 5,000-year-old medical system from ancient India known as Ayurveda* "the knowledge of life span" in Sanskrit." *Perfect Health* went on to describe how to apply the ancient wisdom of Ayurveda to everyday life.

I was so intrigued and inspired by Deepak's approach to the mind and body described in *Perfect Health* that I became a Certified (Deepak) Chopra Perfect Health Instructor. As an instructor, I teach the tools and techniques that are uniquely designed to fit the individual's current and specific needs, focusing on alignment

> *"Wish – Each time I meet someone, I will silently wish them happiness, joy and laughter."*
> *-Deepak Chopra*

and restoring daily life balance. This includes but not limited to:

> ➤ Identify and understand the individual's mind-body constitution
> ➤ What we eat – incorporate the six tastes: specific foods that pacify or aggravates an individual's mind-body constitution. This can be on a daily or seasonal basis
> ➤ The 24-hour day: being in sync, harmony, and rhythm with the day/night, seasonal changes, solar/lunar
> ➤ Emotional Health and Wellbeing: Thrive through the daily stressors. Cultivate happiness from within
> ➤ Inner Pharmacy: Utilizing the five senses for optimal health. Fostering a daily self-care practice
> ➤ Check up after a month and seasonally

If an outside professional is required: together, we can work in tandem with everyone involved, or recommend that the person seek other private individual professional help, based on identifiable special circumstances.

*Note: In Ayurveda terms (Ayurveda = 5000-year-old "science of life" healing system), Dosha of Vata, Pitta, and Kapha = mind-body constitution.

LAUGHTER YOGA

Do you remember the funny class cut-up who made everyone laugh, always interrupting the normal educational thought process of the class by pulling a prank, telling a joke, or making a funny face? Some of those funny class cutups

> "The human race has only one real weapon and that is laughter."
> -Mark Twain

went on to become some of the world's most highly paid and successful comedians of today because early in life, they understood the power of making people laugh!

There are countless comedians from generation to generation, who have all impacted our lives using their ability to make us laugh, and laugh we did! On your note pad; make a list of the comedians that made you laugh, and laugh, and laugh. From stand-up comedy live on stage, to television sitcom comedy shows. You can add A-List motion picture stars on the big screen, or maybe it was a family member or friend. I'm sure when you are writing your list, you will indeed smile and laugh. Now continue reading once your list is complete.

LAUGHTER YOGA DISCUSSION

Laughter Yoga is different from stand-up comedy. However, the one critical element that both disciplines share is the ability to bring laughter to your soul. Laughter Yoga is a discipline and technique specifically designed to generate physiological and psychological benefits to the mind and body.

Before I dive into the art of Laughter Yoga, read what some other well-known and highly successful people think about the importance of laughter:

> ➤ *Walt Disney – "Laughter is America's most important export."*
> ➤ *Charles Dickens – "There is nothing in the world so irresistibly contagious as laughter and good humor."*
> ➤ *George Bernard Shaw – "Life does not cease to be funny when people die any more than it ceases to be serious when people laugh."*
> ➤ *Stephen King – "Anything that has the power to make you laugh over thirty years later isn't a waste of time. I think something like that is very close to immortality."*

Laughter Yoga celebrated it's 25th anniversary in 2019. Dr. Madan and Madhuri Kataria founded Laughter Yoga, blending yoga breathing techniques with playful laughter exercises.

According to Laughter Yoga University, the concept of Laughter Yoga is based on a scientific fact that the body cannot differentiate between fake and real laughter. One gets the same physiological and psychological benefits. Clinical research conducted in Bangalore, India and in the United States has proved that laughter lowers the level of stress hormones (epinephrine, cortisol, etc.) in the blood.

5 BENEFITS OF LAUGHTER YOGA:

1. Good Mood and More Laughter: Laughter Yoga helps to change your mood within minutes by releasing certain chemicals from your brain cells called endorphins. You will remain cheerful and in a good mood throughout the day and will laugh more than you normally do.

"I'm happy that I have brought laughter because I have been shown by many the value of it in so many lives, in so many ways."
-Lucille "I Love Lucy" Ball

2. Healthy Exercise to Beat Stress: Laughter Yoga is like an aerobic exercise (cardio workout) which brings more oxygen to the body and brain thereby making one feel more energetic and relaxed.
3. Health Benefits: Laughter Yoga reduces stress and strengthens the immune system. You will not fall sick easily, and if you have some chronic health conditions, you will heal (in some case studies) faster.
4. Quality of Life: Laughter is a positive energy which helps people to connect with other people quickly and improves relationships. If you laugh more, you will attract many friends.
5. Positive Attitude in Challenging Times: Everyone can laugh when life is good, but how does one laugh when faced with challenges? Laughter helps to create a positive mental state to deal with negative situations and negative people. It gives hope and optimism to cope with difficult times.

As a Certified Laughter Yoga Leader and Teacher, I've seen first-hand the benefits of laughter yoga. Here are some of the tools and techniques used in a Laughter Yoga session:

➤ Warm up stretches
➤ Yoga breathing techniques
➤ 10 - 15 Laughter Yoga exercises (there are 40 foundational exercises, and hundreds of universally created exercises globally).
➤ Cool down exercises and returning to at rest (normal) breathing
➤ Taught on a daily or weekly bases to groups or individuals
➤ Can be taught in person, on the phone, on Skype/FaceTime, or recorded viewing options

> *"Laughter heals all wounds, and that's the one thing that everybody shares. No matter what you're going through, it makes you forget about your problems. I think the world should keep laughing."*
>
> *-Kevin Hart*

➤ Self-massage instruction
➤ Silent Laughter exercise
➤ Seasonal Change (one technique)
➤ Sessions last from 30 to 90 minutes

Laughter Yoga Sessions for Corporate Wellness and Team Building (30, 45, 60 or 90-minute sessions).

➤ Using similar techniques as listed above, with a few additions for employees to use while sitting at their desk
➤ Taught as a one time, or on a reoccurring weekly or monthly bases
➤ Taught during lunch hour, during the business day, or extended corporate day

I'm also certified to teach individuals to become Certified Laughter Yoga Leaders. If you are interested in Laughter Yoga Certification, contact me for a free consultation and my Leader Certification Program.

When was the last time you had a gut-busting stress relieving laugh? How about starting right NOW! Find a Laughter Yoga video on the internet. Watch one of the videos and have yourself a good laugh. For personal instruction; you can contact me.

Robert Frost – "If we couldn't laugh, we would all go insane."

Thank You Amy

THE REFLECTION OF SELF IN THE GLASS MIRROR

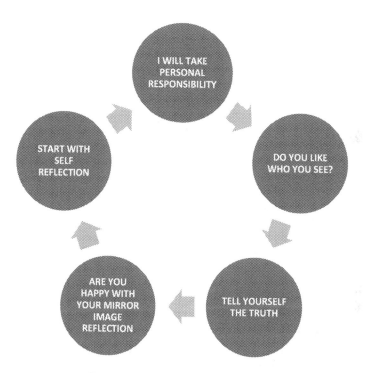

By Michael Bart Mathews

T he mind of the man or woman in the mirror that is staring back at you is very powerful. It can make you or break you. It can talk you into success. It can talk you into failure. It can talk you into marriage. It can talk you into divorce. It can talk you into being rich. It can talk you into being poor. The mind of the man or woman in the mirror can do what some might think as being impossible. But for those who believe, they know that anything is possible because of how you think, act and feel.

Belief is having unwavering faith in your ideas and gaining the necessary knowledge from doing your due diligence. Identifying the goals and dreams that are in line with your visions and your heart's burning desire is paramount. Taking action will help the man or woman in the mirror to facilitate a positive change from within, before that change can be displayed in your everyday activities.

> *"I'm starting with the man in the mirror, I'm asking him to change his ways, and no message could have been any clearer, if you want to make this world a better place, and then make a change."*
> -Song by Michael Jackson
> -Written by Siedah Garrett & Glen Ballard

If you want to make yourself become a better person and make this world become a better place, look in the mirror of your soul and ask yourself; how is that person really doing? What personal development changes can I make? I'm talking about the one and only reflection that is staring back at you in the mirror!

Do you realize that the self-reflection from the man or woman in the mirror that you see staring back at you is a potent energy source? Look around at all the many successful people who decided to grab the bull of life by its horns and ride it until success was achieved.

They never took time to saddle up, they knew their WHY [reason or purpose-goal or dream] when choosing the correct bull (vision) to ride. Early on, they decided to just do it. Some will, some won't, some do, some don't! Success is just a decision away!

When you unlock that door and discover your moment of positive mental clarity, it will have a profound impact on your growth and personal development for the self-reflection of the man or woman that is staring back at you in the mirror.

Give yourself positive affirmations when you stand in front of the mirror, repeat these words several times; "If it's meant to be, it's up to me." Those are nine of the most powerful words on the planet if you want to transform, change and achieve success in your life.

By combining those nine powerful words together, like the members of a think tank or mastermind group of like-minded people, the strangest experience suddenly occurs. You begin to feel as though you really can do it! As you repeat those nine powerful words out loud, (if it's meant to be, it's up to me) together, over and over again, you begin to form a more positive self-reflection mirror image of yourself, by speaking and hearing your own words in the form of autosuggestion.

You are guiding your mind into thinking more positive thoughts while requesting yourself to take action. "If it's meant to be" means, first you must define what "It" is. "It's up to me" means, the act of you taking action or making a transformational change and no longer staying the same. Once you know what "It" is that you want to accomplish! "It" could mean getting out of debt, starting a new job, a new business startup, a new product or service, or improving an existing product or service by twenty-five percent. Whatever "It" is, you first must clearly define "It," in order to achieve "It."

Now write your own list of at least ten positive affirmations below or on a separate note pad, that you will memorize and repeat out loud when you wake up in the morning and retire before going to bed at night. Also, re-read the positive affirmations provided by Karel Vermeulen in Chapter 9. Stand in front of the mirror while staring at your reflection and watch yourself as you are speaking these words. Next, post your affirmations on the mirror, on the refrigerator, on your computer, and on your cellphone screen saver. Keep a copy in your wallet or purse for quick review during challenging times of thought. The more you can see and read your list, the more times you verbally repeat your list out loud, the faster your positive affirmations will become ingratiated into your conscious and subconscious mind. As you grow and change, so should your list.

HERE IS THE LIST OF TEN OF MY FAVORITE POSITIVE SELF-AFFIRMATIONS. I USED THESE REGULARLY:

1. How I think, feel and act is the key to my destiny/I will laugh more.
2. I will always reach out, dream big, and believe in myself.
3. The Best Improvement Starts with Self Improvement.
4. Change is not change until I change.
5. I'm using the attitude of gratitude, being thankful for where I am in life today.
6. I'm not in a race with anyone else, the only thing that matters is that I cross the finish line.
7. If it's meant to be, it's up to me/don't sweat the small stuff.
8. I'm a winner, can't nobody steal my dream.
9. I will persist until I succeed/if you fail to plan-you plan to fail.
10. My success is because of the progressive realization of worthy ideas & action.

Each one of us has the ability to take the high road, beginning with one single idea. There is no doubt that success can be achieved by everyone. The question is, what price are you willing to pay to achieve success? Are you willing to legally, morally and ethically do whatever it takes? Imagine experiencing the kind of success that some people will never personally experience. Many of those same people will sit in front of the television and watch reality T.V. shows day-in-and-day-out. They sometimes criticize you for going full-out to achieve "that special something" that you seek.

The Universe is vast and has yet to uncover its full potential. We have not discovered our full potential, just like the man or woman staring back at you in the mirror. There are always people to see, places to go, and things to do for those who climb the staircase of life, one step at a time. There is never a final top step to success. The sky has no limits, depending on how you think, act and feel about the peak potential of the self-reflection staring back at you in the mirror of life.

Practice looking at your self-reflection in the mirror more frequently throughout the day. I don't mean taking selfies for social media. Are you happy with your self-reflection, the one that you see in the mirror that's always staring back at you? Do you see a go-getter, a mover and a shaker, a shark? Do you see a very confident person who is going after his or her goals, dreams and visions?

Or do you see the self-reflection of a man or woman who has low self-esteem? Do you see the self-reflection of a man or woman who has several emotional baggage blockers that are preventing you from transformation, change, and success? How often do you look for any reason to blame someone or something else for your shortcomings?

Look back inside of the mind of the man or woman that's staring back at you in the mirror of life. Have you ever had an idea to create or improve a product or service and did nothing? Have you ever looked around and YOUR idea was now the creation of someone else who made the decision to take action, then used the speed of implementation and actually created that product or service? Now today, YOUR idea is making someone else money while providing a good, quality product and or service to the marketplace. Why? Because you failed to take action on your worthy idea! Fear and procrastination are the true assassins of millions of good creative worthy ideas that go nowhere.

Where are some of the greatest ideas in the world? In the cemetery! Most people die, and their dreams are buried with them. If you fail to act upon your ideas right now while you are walking, talking, living and breathing, one day and you can count on it, they will forever be lost upon your death.

Think about thought leaders like; Henry Ford, and Madame CJ Walker who acted upon their ideas. And for decades, long after their death, their original ideas have contributed to multiple generations living a better quality of life because their ideas were turned into a product or service. That is the true definition of leaving a legacy. What legacy will the mind of the man or woman staring back at you leave? What will you be remembered for?

What can you do to make the person who is staring back at you in the mirror change his or her thoughts, feelings and actions toward accomplishment?

It all starts with the mind of the man or woman in the mirror who is staring back at you. Is that person a couch potato or a go-getter? If you think you can, you can, if you think you can't, you can't. Either way, you're right.

Once you start with the man or woman in the mirror and become completely honest with your self-reflection, changes in many areas of your life can occur. This may sound simple but, once you become sick and tired of being sick and tired about the same old thing, you will be closer to *"Finding Your Moment of Clarity!"*

Now is the time to plan and take action. If you are waiting for what you consider to be the right time to get started, you've already lost! The time is right here-right now-today!

Read on to continue your journey!

CHAPTER 11
POSITIVE AFFIRMATION EXERCISE

On your note pad or below, write down at least 10 positive affirmations that will get and keep you energized and motivated throughout your day. Put them in various places; home, office, car, phone, where they will be visible and easily accessible when you need them.

1. _____

2. _____

3. _____

4. _____

5. _____

6. _____

7. _____

8. _____

9. _____

10. _____

CHAPTER 12

WHAT STRESS CAN TEACH YOU ABOUT POWER, RESILIENCE AND EMOTIONAL MASTERY

Allow me, to introduce you, to my good
friends, Peter Diaz & Emi Golding
By Peter Diaz and Emi Golding

M elanie sits across the room, a highly intelligent, highly capable and successful young woman. By all measures of success, she is rocking it – great job, nice apartment, good social life. And yet, she's sitting here in the psychologist's office, seeking help. She feels anxious, stressed, out of control. She wants to know how she can better manage her time, how she can achieve "work-life balance," how to do "self-care" better.

Sadly, we see more and more people like Melanie in our clinic and in our resilience building and mental health workshops. High achievers, smart, A-type professionals, often self-confessed perfectionists with great careers and even better prospects, but they are starting to drop the ball because of stress. They are beginning to make mistakes, underperform, and are starting to question if they are in the right job or business, and how they are going to keep going at this rate. They are on the brink of burnout.

By the way, had you asked them last year, some of these A players and high achievers would not have believed they would be the ones feeling overwhelmed and stressed. It can creep up on you if you're not careful.

No doubt stress can be pernicious. Billions of people around the world would willingly agree with that statement. Trillions are spent every year in healthcare alone in an attempt to either minimise stress itself or the consequences of stress. The problem is stress can permeate every area of life, personal and work. But what is stress, specifically?

STRESS, BEAUTIFUL STRESS

Stress is a natural response to external and internal stimuli. There are numerous definitions out there, but we like this one from *Stress|Psychology Today*: 'the psychological perception of pressure, on the one hand, and the body's response to it, on the other, which involves multiple systems, from metabolism to muscles to memory. Some stress is necessary for all living systems.'

So 'stress' is a 'psychological perception.' That means, it is your brain passing judgment on something. An interpretation.

From this, we can deduce the following: stress is the reaction you have when your brain has judged, interpreted, a certain event or situation as potentially threatening.

Now that's interesting, isn't it? Because if your brain judges a situation, perceives it, as non 'bad,' non-threatening, then it doesn't create stress. It creates something else totally different. It can be joy, excitement, pleasure, surprise, etc. Same situation, completely different result.

Think about it this way. Have you ever been given something you didn't expect? If you liked it, then you called it a 'surprise.' But if you didn't like it, you probably called it a 'problem.' The difference? Your brain judged it as either good or bad for you. Hence the result.

The irony is that you can't get rid of stress. Nor is it desirable you get rid of stress even if you could. Why? Because stress can be good for you. We just don't tend to notice when it is. We take it for granted. Think of stress as a natural, inbuilt mechanism designed to protect you. It is working alongside you all the time. Helping you grow. Creating pleasure. Creating pain. Protecting and safeguarding you.

Remember Spiderman? Stress is like a 'Spidey sense' we have that warns us that something is either wrong or has the potential to go wrong. Pretty cool, right? So, we want stress. We don't want to get rid of it. The aim is to befriend it and learn to communicate with it, use it, in such a way that it starts working for us not against us.

LET STRESS BECOME YOUR TEACHER

Since stress is the result of our psychological interpretation, the meaning we make about an event, then what if we considered stress simply as a 'teacher.' What if stress was your psyche's way of saying 'something isn't right here... you need to re-align'. This is in fact, what many schools of psychology actually say.

You could compare it to a physical health issue. When you feel physical pain, that is your body's way of letting you know that you should stop doing whatever you are doing, or else more severe physical damage will occur. The same can be true of emotional or mental pain. Emotional or mental pain (stress) shows up to let us know we need to stop doing something the way we are doing it and find a new way; or else...So, it is just simply smart, logical and wise that we invite Stress to become our teacher. Let's explore some of the lessons Stress can teach us.

WHAT CAN STRESS TEACH US ABOUT POWER?

Viewed this way, stress can teach us just how much power we actually have, and how to take charge of our own personal power. Let us specify here, that when we say 'power,' we are not talking about power *over others*, but we are talking about *power to* have agency in our lives.

Often, we feel stressed because we feel like we are out of control. In fact, a common symptom of all mental disorders is feeling out of control and powerless. Think about it – we get mad when we feel we have been wronged, and there is nothing we can do about it – no avenue of recourse. We feel sad when we think we have lost something and there is nothing we can do to get it back. We feel anxious when we are worried about and feel we can't control, what might happen in the future. When we focus on what we CAN do, we feel calmer, less stressed, and more in control of ourselves.

In our "Resilience At Work" masterclass, we teach participants about the four powers we each have. Namely, the four (and only four) powers we have, are the powers of our words, actions, thoughts, and feelings. Most people can fairly easily understand and accept the first two – that only I can control what I say and do. After all, they are *my* words – no one else makes me say anything, and no one else makes me do anything. They may try to influence me, they can even hold a gun to my head, but it is up to me how I will respond in that scenario.

But it is often the second two that people have trouble with – I have power over my thoughts and feelings. That one can be a bit harder. 'Sometimes it feels like thoughts just pop into my head.' Yes, it's true you may not yet have mastered how to control your own thoughts and manage them effectively, but they are still *your* thoughts, no one else put them in there, no one else thought it for you. *You* did that. And the same with feelings. No one else *made you* angry. *You* chose to feel angry. Perhaps they did or said something that violated your standards, but nevertheless, *you* responded by feeling angry. That was *your* feeling.

Even more important than that, is the distinction that we only have power over our OWN words, actions, thoughts, and feelings, but not anyone else's.

That can be a relief for some – 'I don't need to worry about anyone else, because, while I can exert influence, I can't control them anyway.' But for others, people who have a strong need to micromanage and control their world around them, that can feel chaotic, and send them into a spin – 'If I can't control, if I don't have power over other people, or over the outside world around me, what if something bad happens?' Here stress teaches us another important lesson – to learn to be comfortable with uncertainty. It's been said that the quality of our life is in direct proportion to the level of uncertainty we can comfortably tolerate. There's some deep truth to that, even if that's not always the case.

Life is uncertain, life is full of surprises. You can't predict the future. And therefore, if we are to have any chance of living with peace, we need to learn to embrace uncertainty, ambiguity, and be at ease in the unknown, or we will continue to create and experience high levels of stress, especially when we are actively engaged in a pursuit that involves other people or external variables.

Some people try to control everything in their world, but they can only do that by keeping their world small. In order to expand, you must take on risks, and to do that you must be able to handle uncertainty. That is personal power. That is what stress teaches us about power.

Interestingly, the research has shown that one of the four essential ingredients for recovery from a mental health issue is 'Responsibility.' Time and time again, people who have recovered from a severe mental disorder have said that their recovery really began once they took responsibility for their own recovery. This doesn't mean that they became boring and serious, got a 9 to 5 job in an office and made sure to brush their teeth and go to bed on time. We're talking about 'Responsibility' in the sense of being response-able. Having the power to choose how to respond to the various situations we face day to day and throughout our lives.

Of course, we don't need to wait until we are so stressed, we develop a disorder, to hopefully take the lesson and begin applying it in our lives. The ongoing meta-question is 'are you teachable'? Many are not so teachable. Most of us are haughty and arrogant. Yet, people who have experienced a degree of success in any human endeavor – both in terms of external achievements and in personal peace and fulfillment and wellbeing, tend to welcome teachers and adopt a lot of personal responsibility and are therefore empowered to be active agents in their own lives.

Used properly, stress is always teaching us where we need to take more responsibility. Where we need to stop playing the role of a powerless 'victim' and embrace our personal power, the role of the 'victor' instead, to choose how we will respond in situations where we cannot control our environment or other people, but we can choose how we will speak, act, think and feel.

[What will you decide to be? Victim or Victor? Ultimately, it's up to you!]

WHAT CAN STRESS TEACH US ABOUT RESILIENCE?

Resilience is commonly described as the ability to 'bounce back,' to face life's challenges, fall down and get back up again. And we agree that this is an important aspect of Resilience. But as we share in our resilience and wellbeing programs, and with our clients, this is just one aspect of resilience.

To use the analogy of falling down and getting back up again, it reminds us of when a baby first learns to walk. They fall down plenty of times, and no parent says, 'look, honey, I just don't think you're going to ever walk – you're just not a walker.' No! We encourage the little one to get up and keep going and try again. That is resilience. But over time, as the child gets better at walking, they also start to fall over less and less. That too is resilience. Things that might have easily tripped them up earlier don't have the same effect anymore. Soon the child starts running. And if you've ever watched a young child learning to walk and run, you'll have seen the times when they catch their foot on something, and just as you are sure they are going to fall, somehow, their little body has learned to adjust. They are able to compensate and accommodate, and they can avoid falling over. This too is resilience. And we think this is an important part. Resilience is not just about getting back up after you fall, it is also about building your capacity, strength, and emotional fitness so that you are less likely to fall in the first place.

And this is what stress teaches us. Without ever being exposed to a challenging situation, how can you possibly build up the emotional fitness necessary? If you've never been uncomfortable, how can you get comfortable with new things? Many of you may be familiar with the idea of the comfort zone. As we slowly start to stretch our comfort zone, we become more capable of handling discomfort without falling apart emotionally. We develop cognitive and emotional strategies so that things which might have once shocked us, angered us, frustrated us, or rocked us, may not even cause a blip on the register. There are countless times you've done this as you grew up over the years. Why stop stretching the comfort zone once you reach a certain age? An appropriate amount of stress helps us to get stronger.

Psychologists know that we cannot, and should not, protect people from the challenges of life. We can't create situations which are 100% safe all of the time, where nothing ever goes wrong, and everything is exactly the way we want it. Even if we could, we shouldn't. It would hurt people. They wouldn't have the space to learn from trial and error. Emotionally speaking, they'd be atrophied, stunted, and unable to face the world. Instead, we need to teach people to handle the realities of life.

For good mental health, rather than remove all potential stressors from our lives, we need to learn to be resilient and to handle stress and cope with it easily, joyfully and effectively. Because to live life means there will be challenges. A life without challenges would actually be rather boring, wouldn't it? Have you ever met a person that had what you wanted but took it for granted? That's what overprotecting someone does. Every positive thing you have in your life – the job, the partner, the house, you have because you took a risk, you stretched your comfort zone.

WHAT CAN STRESS TEACH US ABOUT EMOTIONAL MASTERY?

And here we come to the crux of the matter. In our experience, the single most important skill a person can develop is the ability to be the master over our emotions, rather than allow them to master us. It is so powerful that it is like a superpower. When a person can say "I am the captain of my ship, and my emotions are the crew, they work for me" that is when a person has real emotional mastery.

If you are able to understand this, then that means that you have come across someone like that at some point in your life or have heard about someone like that. For us, Nelson Mandela was like that. Not the Nelson Mandela that went into prison, immature, ready to kill people, but the Nelson Mandela that came out of prison after 27 years. No bitterness, ready to build people up of any race. That's emotional mastery! But, if he doesn't do it for you, that's ok, who's that person that matches this description of an emotional master for you?

Too often people fall victim to their emotions. If the emotions are the crew, they have mutinied and started running the ship. The captain may be saying 'Hey guys, I want to go over here, in this direction, this is what I want to do,' but the emotions are running the show, and taking the ship in every which way direction, except the one the captain wanted. To be captain of my ship, master of my emotions, I need to step up as a Leader. Emotions can give me valuable information or feedback on when I may be off course, or there is something else to attend to, but they work for me. They are my servants, my staff, not the other way around.

In our "Resilience At Work" courses around the world, we often meet stressed people with a common story. A story of busyness, overwhelm and anxiety. Within one day, these same people walk out of the workshops smiling, relaxed and just a tad taller than when they came in. They've had a conscious taste of mastery. They've collectively learned to leverage stress to reach new heights of personal power, resilience in the face of life and professional challenges. How is that even possible? Because the psychological principles and techniques shown in our "Resilience At Work" course deeply respect how our brains work. These principles and techniques work with your brain to generate the kinds of actions and feelings needed to succeed in living a truly successful and meaningful life.

Can you imagine what your life will be like as this happens? What a difference, right? Not only in terms of your productivity and efficacy at work or your bottom line if you're in business, but more importantly, your health, wellbeing and that of your family and friends around you.

This is something we spoke about recently with Randi Zuckerberg, Mark Zuckerberg's sister, of Facebook fame, and the former Director of Marketing for Facebook. In such a fast paced, high pressure and high-performance environment like Facebook, the importance of building Resilience is something she was incredibly passionate about. And that's because she saw the impact it had on the workforce. You can watch our interview by going to the Workplace Mental Health Institute's YouTube Channel.

https://www.youtube.com/user/TheMHRI

Thank you for listening to us. We know these principles work. Why? We've experienced the first-hand results of thousands of people who have been through our workshops. That's why we know this information is sacred, and that it changes lives for the best. We also wish that for you.

An Irish Blessing: "May the road rise to meet you. May the wind be always at your back. May the sun shine warm upon your face. May the rain fall soft upon your fields."

Thank You Peter & Emi

THE MAGICAL POWER OF YOUR THOUGHTS

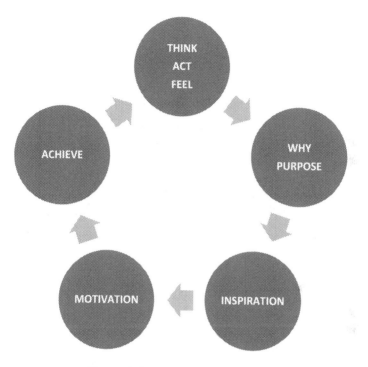

By Michael Bart Mathews

It's time to see how you think, feel, and act about life, liberty and the pursuit of transformation, happiness, and success. Think about changing some things in your life as you discover your magical power from within? In this chapter you will find several different antidotes, which have the ability to counteract the voice of overwhelm that fills your head with negative thoughts and feelings of helplessness, hopelessness, disbelief, and discontentment. Thoughts of not being good enough, unworthiness, low self-esteem, feeling like a failure and most importantly, declutter your stinkin thinkin!

Imagine you have completely changed your self-imposed bad or destructive habits, with new and success driven habits. Let's also add, that you are no longer a powerless victim. You can master your emotions and embrace your power.

So far, you read about and may have already put into practice, discovering why you are here on earth and what your purpose is. What the power of motivation can do for you. What it means to be in the vortex while finding balance. Awaken to Your Soul along your journey was discussed. You also read the *Art of Meditation* and the *Art of Laughter Yoga* for improving mental clarity. Then you learned about stress, resilience, emotional mastery, and the four powers; 1. Words, 2. Thoughts, 3. Actions, 4. Feelings.

And most importantly, you read about the impact that the mirror image, self-reflection process for change has on the mind of the man or woman that is staring back at you.

On the following pages, you will have the opportunity to self-diagnose your own interpretation and understanding of how you currently think, act and feel about the power of your thoughts. You will have the opportunity to self-reflect on your answers that are coming directly from your thoughts, experiences and life journey. This will provide you with a better understanding and interpretation of yourself.

There is no wrong answer! You cannot fail! This will help you increase your own self-awareness, personal growth and development, self-improvement, and self-actualization in the areas of your choosing. Write down your thoughts to the best of your ability. The secret sauce is for you to be 100% honest with yourself as you answer each question. Now it's time to weed out your fantasies, and begin to face your fears, and start living in your reality!

This personal growth and development self-help exercise will give you a better gage or benchmark as to what changes you can make for yourself in your home-life and within your work-life. You will point yourself in the direction of transformation using your own answers that come from how you think, act and feel!

You can reread any section in this book as many times as you like. Use whatever reference points that will allow you to be 100% honest with yourself and get rid of your fantasies and embrace reality.

Millions of people around the globe are walking around carrying a heavy load of mentally, self-imposed, self-destructive, emotion-filled baggage blockers. They allow these baggage blockers to hold themselves back from obtaining their own personal and business success. Stop Now! Think for a moment. What mentally, self-imposed, self-destructive emotional baggage blockers can you identify that are currently holding you back? What can you do to release and let them go, or keep them in your rear-view mirror giving them little or no focus?

> *"The Best Improvement Starts With Self Improvement."*
> *-Michael Bart Mathews*

Sort through your mind, identify the mentally, self-imposed, self-destructive emotional baggage blockers that feel like a ton of bricks resting on your shoulders of progress. Examples of some mentally, self-imposed, self-destructive emotional baggage blockers:

➤ I am not good enough
➤ The voice of overwhelm
➤ I can't do it
➤ I'm afraid
➤ I'm too old
➤ I don't look good enough
➤ I'm not smart enough
➤ Things have always been this way
➤ They were born rich

➤ I was born poor

To begin the process of decluttering your thoughts, write down your list of mentally, self-imposed, self-destructive emotional baggage blocker's that you want to get rid of. Put today's date at the top of the list and sign your name at the bottom of the list.

Now that you have identified your list of mentally, self-imposed, self-destructive emotional baggage blockers, it's time to face your fantasies or fears, as you begin to omit them from your thought process and daily actions. You will begin to transform negative thoughts, feelings, and actions into positive, self-gratifying, rewarding results.

To help you accomplish this, it's also time to change your past or current bad habits and replace them with new and good habits. Once you are able to change your thoughts, you will also change your feelings. When you are able to change your beliefs, your emotions also will change. You now have the power to change your actions which are connected to changing your habits! Do not allow the voice of overwhelm to derail you off track.

This will help you to discover the Magic of Thinking Big, as you begin to become more aware and build more confidence. You can begin to transform how you think, act and feel in the present, by changing your past habits. This will also help you to develop a more optimistic outlook towards your future.

Expand the list, identify as many mentally, self-imposed, self-destructive emotional baggage blockers as you can. Work on the I can, rather than the I can't theory in any and all endeavors that you undertake. I invite you to reflect back on any or all of the co-contributing authors and utilize their methodologies toward transformation in the specific areas that best fit what you write down. They all have submitted a treasure trove of useful information highly capable of providing you with the necessary results that you seek.

Once you have completed this exercise, remember, every co-author also has the ability to coach you along your journey.

Again, once and for all, get rid of your fantasies and start living in your reality.

CHAPTER 13
POWER OF YOUR THOUGHTS EXERCISE

On your note pad or below, write down at least five emotional baggage blockers that you believe are standing in the way of you moving forward towards making positive changes in your life.

1. _____

2. _____

3. _____

4. _____

5. _____

Also, write down at least five steps or changes you can make, that you believe can help to eliminate those emotional baggage blockers. Give this some serious thought. If you need help, then seek it from a professional or someone you trust.

1. _____

2. _____

3. _____

4. _____

5. _____

THE POWER IN THE MAGIC OF THINKING BIG

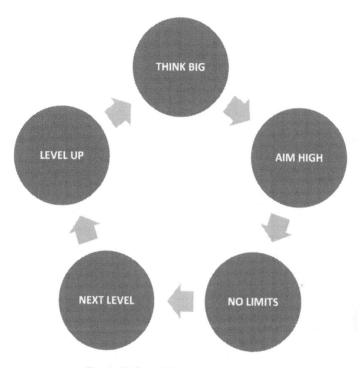

By Michael Bart Mathews

The Power in the *Magic of Thinking Big*, will also give you that much needed expansion of your mind. This concept was first introduced to me by a man named David Schwartz, the author of the *Magic of Thinking Big*. Once the mind has been expanded, it is almost impossible for it to return back to its normal size. Mind expansion means for you to reach out, dream big, then dream bigger and bigger and bigger!

Let's make no mistake about dreams. Without realistic, written, attainable goals, research, and due diligence, most importantly, taking the necessary action toward accomplishment, and never quitting, a dream will always be just a cloud or a puff of smoke in the distance!

The higher you climb up the mountain, the thinner the air quality becomes. The higher you climb up the ladder of success, the less crowded life becomes. The bigger you think, the bigger the possibilities. The bigger the possibilities, the more action you should take. The more action you take, the more opportunities for achieving results are present. Imagine you are willing to roll up your mental sleeves and begin the process of learning the benefits that will come from harnessing the power from the *Magic of Thinking Big*.

Most people are not willing to keep their mental ear to the ground and their nose to the grindstone; meaning they don't or won't take time out to stop and think big thoughts and listen to their inner mind and allow it to guide them. Do you think big thoughts, or do you think small thoughts! Either way, the Universe will deliver to your doorstep what it is that you think. So why not think big!

Your thoughts have the power to help while you are *"Finding Your Moment of Clarity." To* help you see clearly as you embark toward achieving your life's bravest journey. That journey is to find out your WHY [reason or purpose - goal or dream] here on planet earth, then plan and take the necessary action steps to achieve it!

Developing the belief in the *Magic of Thinking Big* is another way of thinking positive thoughts toward or about yourself, and about others. Thinking Big in all areas of your life will forever transform how you see yourself and the world, once you have dismissed your past small thinking.

What do I mean by small thinking? Have you ever experienced talking yourself out of doing something that you knew you wanted to accomplish? Like a rookie basketball player competing for a starting spot on a professional basketball team. He had an excellent college career and gets drafted in the first round. He's all pumped up after completing rookie camp and ready to go. Then he walks into the locker room and sees the seasoned, all pro veteran, who happens to be starting at the same position he is competing for.

Out of nowhere, that inner voice (the voice of overwhelm), that small thinking rears its ugly head filled with negativity. It literally talked the rookie out of being the best that he can be. In other cases, that same rookie accepts the challenge, plays his or her heart out and becomes the starter. The same is true for you and me in the game of life, only if you allow it to happen. You can be the starter or the bench warmer in the daily game of life.

Of course, the young, inexperienced rookie dismissed the fear of failure and went on to become one of the NBA or WNBA's marquee players because he or she faced his or her fears head-on. They also benefited from having a talented, experienced coach to hold them accountable toward success. Just as you can go on and become the marquee player in the game of life with the business model of your choice. Just like championship basketball teams have a thought leader called COACH, in the game of life, championship business owners also have access to a thought leader called COACH!

To some degree, we all experienced small thinking and the Magic of Thinking Big, even when we did not realize the true nature of both thought processes.

Let's mentally time travel back into the past for a moment. Remember back to our high school or teenage years. There is a particular experience that a vast majority of people can relate to. Have a laugh and smile about this one!

EXAMPLE OF SMALL THINKING:

Remember when you were an inexperienced young man or young lady, and you saw what you believed to be the most beautiful person in the world standing across the room at the dance. He or she was everything that your heart desired. There was one problem; you began to think small thoughts like, maybe I'm not good enough, what if I walk all the way across the room and get rejected? What if his or her friends laugh at me? That will feel like a long walk of shame back if I strike out?

So, you gazed at him or her from afar never taking the first step. You never knew what he or she would have said because you talked yourself out (small thinking) of approaching and introducing yourself. You allowed the voice of overwhelm to win. Later on, you found out they were hoping that you would come over and ask them to dance! A missed opportunity because you did not take action because of small thinking.

EXAMPLE OF THE POWER IN THE *MAGIC OF THINKING BIG*:

You saw that same beautiful person across the room at the dance. You immediately began to use The Magic of Thinking Big. You made sure he or she noticed you from afar. You took the casual stroll across the room and introduced yourself, not once worrying about being rejected or embarrassed. You made small talk until the right song came on. You asked him or her to dance and low and behold you succeed. You brought about what you thought about, and that was to meet him or her and get that dance. And the best part, as you were dancing, you heard a whisper in your ear, "I was hoping you would ask me to dance." After the song was over, you proudly strutted instead of walking back across the room to your click of friends who were still standing together. They did not face their fear and did not ask anyone for a dance. You held your head up a little higher and developed some swagger. You now held a bit more status within your click or group, because you took action.

Why was this example a success? Because from the outset, your Thinking was so Big, you knew that you would succeed! You believe it, you took action and walked across the room and introduced yourself. The rest was history. Now think about your teenaged inexperience and the more confident you became with each new experience. The same is true today. Experience in the game of life breeds confidence, and confidence breeds success.

As you think back and relate to the two examples of thinking small and The Magic of Thinking Big, it's a concept for success that's been around for a very long time. The Magic of Thinking Big can be used for anything that your heart desires; for example:

- ➤ The person you choose for your life partner
- ➤ The job you seek
- ➤ The business you start up
- ➤ The clothes you wear
- ➤ The community you live in
- ➤ The house you live in
- ➤ The car you drive
- ➤ The trips you take
- ➤ The level of education you aspire to complete
- ➤ The amount of money you aspire to accumulate
- ➤ The number of people you decide to help
- ➤ The people you associate with

The list can go on and on and on! Once you understand the importance of dismissing small thoughts, defeating the voice of overwhelm and adapting the philosophy of The Magic of Thinking Big, your mind will never be the same. You will learn and understand that your thoughts can become your success. You can program your mind into delivering positive thoughts of affirmation when you use the principal centered Magic of Thinking Big concept.

Don't forget, along with The Magic of Thinking Big, you are most certainly required to take action to attain any desired results from your thinking!

CHAPTER 14
THINKING BIG THOUGHTS EXERCISE

To reinforce and focus your thinking, write the following list in your note pad or below; I will use The Magic of Thinking Big in the following areas:

1. Building successful personal & business relationships.
2. Self-actualization, personal growth & development.
3. Financial matters.
4. Service to others.
5. Creating products & services/business building.

1. _____

2. _____

3. _____

4. _____

5. _____

Now take some time and expand your list or start from scratch and come up with a list of your own.

1. _____

2. _____

3. _____

4. _____

5. _____

CHAPTER 15

LISTEN TO YOUR NEW INNER VOICE

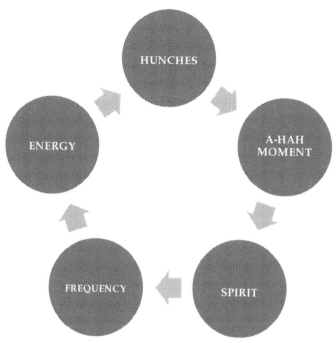

By Michael Bart Mathews

A s you are strolling through your mind, still listening to that inner voice that talks to you? It's your internal guidance system, intuition or gut feeling. It can hold you back from or allow you to live "Your Purpose Driven Life." It can lead you down the path of greatness, righteousness, results, and success, as you walk your life's bravest journey.

Now is the time to stop the "Stinkin Thinkin!" Not yesterday, not tomorrow, NOW! Listen to your new inner voice, tap into your positive internal guiding system filled with an abundance of illuminating energy.

Be aware of the energy field that surrounds your everyday positive or negative thoughts. Imagine you have learned how to tap into the positive internal energy source of thought. Think about you being energized as your guiding light shines bright, as you discover your power within. Think about what a difference it will make when you find your moment of clarity that clearly outlines introspective transformation, personal growth and development within your life.

Imagine you have reclaimed your positive mental attitude of thought and you are now experiencing change and success. Think about your personality change that assisted you in developing new habits. Like the ones displayed by highly successful people. Imagine putting into practice any or all of the many habits of highly effective people can and will enhance your belief of positive transformation.

That inner voice or internal guidance system inside is one reason why things do or don't go as planned. When you have private conversations with yourself, you must take charge of your mind, and dispel the guidance from that negative inner voice. Begin to use the Power of Positive Thinking and replace those negative thoughts with positivity.

> *"Principles are natural laws that are external to us and ultimately control the consequences of our actions. Values are internal and subjective and represent that which we feel strongest about in guiding our behavior."*
> *-Steven Covey*

While searching and *"Finding Your Moment of Clarity,"* you will develop a certain rhythm, a special kind of vibe or quest for making positive change occur in your life. By adopting many different habits of some highly successful and effective people, you can accomplish the desired results that you seek. You have the power right now, right here today, to take advantage of the plethora of new possibilities that can manifest in your life.

That friend inside of your head (that positive inner voice) can add value and will transform you to believe that the possibility of "now or today" clearly out weights and is more important than yesterday and tomorrow! You can't change what happen yesterday or in the past. You can plan for tomorrow or the future. But you must embrace the thought of living now, today, in the present moment. The direction of your thoughts today will determine the outcome of your existence tomorrow and beyond!

You can achieve maximum, positive change and success within your life. While you are taking one of life's bravest journey's, it is very important for you to learn *"How to Win Friends and Influence People"* from all walks of life. The Universe provides us with like-minded people who first were strangers. Like the fast blink of the human eye, the two strangers became friends.

That voice inside your head, that positive value-added inner voice, learn how to take charge and allow your thoughts to deflect all negativity from the conversations that you have with yourself! Our thoughts determine who we really are, how we act, what we really want, and where we want to go in life. Our thoughts determine how we think, act, and feel. Our thoughts are our destiny!

I'm not talking about the kind of thinking that will require you to be put into a locked padded cell with both arms tied up behind your back in a white straight jacket, while in a controlled environment. I'm talking about the regular, daily conversations from thoughts that you draw upon to assist you in the typical day in and day out process of decision making.

Bar none, it's a proven fact, that the man or woman who can take charge of their mind and develop a positive mental attitude about themselves will begin to see more opportunities that life has to offer. You have the power to guide how you think, act, and feel by way of positive or negative thought. The choice is for you to make!

I encourage you to take a stroll through your mind, and declutter and clear the cobwebs of negativity, and illuminate your new, improved, positive thoughts from your mind.

You can find your acres of diamonds within the rubbish pile of stinking thinking. It all depends on how you think about what you're looking for, and how badly you want it! Will you recognize it when you see it?

The rarest of diamonds all have something in common, the 4C's, better known as GIA standards for quality and perfection within each cut.

1. Color
2. CLARITY
3. Cut
4. Carat Weight

The 4C's of diamond quality is a technique or method used for assessing the quality of diamonds anywhere in the world! Remember when you went shopping for your wedding rings, or that diamond bracelet, the jeweler or trained gemologist picked up the looking glass while explaining the 4C's to you. While *Finding Your Moment of Clarity*, color, and cut, you viewed the diamond through the looking glass.

Consider your brain to be your very own hope size diamond. Within your thoughts are your acres of diamonds. The one thing that you want to identify should be at least one of the 4C's of assessing diamonds, which is CLARITY.

Using the voice in your head, directing it with clarity introspectively in the mirror of self-reflection, you can achieve your heart's desire.

REDEFINING F.E.A.R.

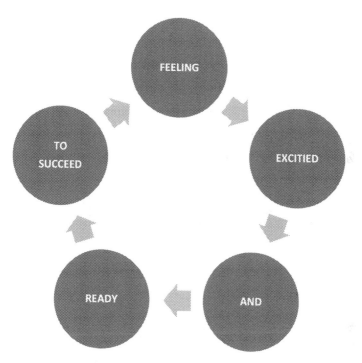

By Michael Bart Mathews

W e briefly touched on the subject of F.E.A.R. Fear often comes from listening to the voice of overwhelm inside of your head. F.E.A.R. has been referred to as False Evidence Appearing Real. While we are not born with fears, as we grow up and are inundated with other people's opinions and beliefs. These opinions and beliefs become our own and often become significant obstacles in achieving our goals, dreams, and desires. Fear can be your biggest emotional baggage blocker.

What makes these emotions surface? Learning how to eliminate fear from your life is one of the most critical personal growth, development, and self-help bravest journeys that you can undertake! There are all kinds of fears and failures that we face every day.

THE MERRIAM-WEBSTER DEFINITION OF FEAR IS:

> To be afraid of something or someone
> To expect or worry about something bad or unpleasant
> To be afraid and worried

"I learned that courage was not the absence of fear, but the triumph over it. The brave man is not he who does not feel afraid, but he who conquers that fear."
  -Nelson Mandela

EXAMPLES OF FEAR ARE:

> The fear of failure
> The fear of public speaking
> The fear of change
> The fear of rejection
> The fear of heights
> The fear of running out of money before the end of each month

Now is the time to face whatever fears that are holding you back. It's time to "REDEFINE" F.E.A.R. as "Face Everything And Rise" or "Feeling Excited And Ready."

"Forget about the consequences of failure. Failure is only a temporary change in direction to set you straight for your next success."
  -Dennis Waitley

People have learned to face their fears and failures head-on. They found out they were really good at the very thing they were once afraid of! The same can happen for you. Take a bold step and begin to do the things that you fear the most, even though you may feel somewhat stressed and uncomfortable. If you need professional coaching to assist you in facing your fears, by all means, seek it. Trust the process, and organically, it will get easier somewhere down the road. Begin to think positive thoughts, walk with your head up, believing that you can do it.

From this moment forward, I urge you to make the paradigm shift away from the old definition of False Evidence Appearing Real, to the new paradigm re-definitions of F.E.A.R. Remember: what we think about, we become!

To help with the re-definition process; start by listening to the positive inner voice that you have developed from taking a stroll through your mind. Give yourself as many positive verbal self-affirmations as needed. You can say things to yourself like:

> For every one of my adversities, I'm going to find my seed of greatness
> It's not what happens to me, it's how I respond to it, that counts
> Winners never quit, quitters never win
> I believe in myself, I can do it
> I may not know this, but I can learn this
> I will plan my work, and I will work my plan
> I do have the Universal power to transform my current situation
> I will develop and keep the attitude of gratitude
> I am very grateful for the blessing that I currently enjoy

"Inaction breeds doubt and FEAR. Action breeds confidence and courage. If you want to conquer FEAR, do not sit home and think about it. Go out and get busy."
-Dale Carnegie

Also, you may need to make some changes in your life to remove yourself from situations, relationships or an environment that supports and feeds your fears. The definition of insanity is to keep doing the same thing and expect a different outcome.

We all have a laundry list full of changes that we know we want or need to make within ourselves. Some examples of things that you can begin to change are, however, not limited to the following:

- Stop complaining
- Stop associating with negative people
- Stop negative thinking
- Accept the things that you know you need to change
- Get out of toxic, unhealthy relationships (personal and business)
- Stop being selfish and start being of service to others
- Stop bullying
- Start your journey of personal development, growth, and self-improvement by utilizing the Five-Hour Rule
- Start getting physically fit by going to the gym, health club, use of a personal trainer, power walking, jogging, etc.
- Get your finances under control-lack of money can be fearful

CHAPTER 16
RE-DEFINE YOUR FEARS EXERCISE

Write down below, or on a separate note pad, the top 5 things that you fear the most in life. Now decide that you are going to face those fears. Do not allow the voice of overwhelm to stop you.

1. _____

2. _____

3. _____

4. _____

5. _____

Now list the top 5 things that you want to change to help you overcome those fears. Remember, change is not change, until you change. Write down your action steps that will start you on your journey of change and overcoming those fears. Seek help, if you need it.

1. _____

2. _____

3. _____

4. _____

5. _____

YOU WERE BORN TO WIN

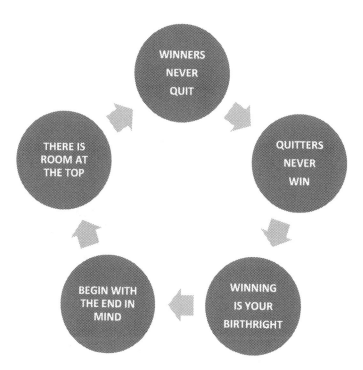

By Michael Bart Mathews

Have you ever seriously thought about how ordinary people have accomplished extraordinary things? The person who was not born with a silver spoon in their mouths. The person who did not benefit from having old money (trust fund/generational wealth). The person who was labeled a failure and would never amount to anything. Yet, that same person, years later, achieved a high level of success.

That was the same person who did not grow up in the best of neighborhoods, did not go to the best schools, did not get the best education compared to the wealthier and more affluent neighborhoods elsewhere. The person who did not have the financial resources to take advantage of cultural experiences like going to museums, theater stage plays or taking trips domestically and abroad. How did they achieve success? Were they just born to win?

> "You were born to win, but to be a winner, you must plan to win, prepare to win, and expect to win."
>
> -Zig Ziglar

There are countless stories of how millions of ordinary people have accomplished extraordinary things. What was the wind beneath their wings that enabled them to soar high like an eagle and experience the kind of success that most people read about, or watch on television or only dream about? Why do some succeed when others fail? Were they just born to win?

Like many successful people, they all experienced their a-ha, this is it, moment of clarity! They all began to understand the positive power of thought. They all found "that special something" to laser focus in on. They all decided they would do what it takes to transform their current circumstances. They decided to do what others won't so they could change how they think, act and feel about the glass of life being half empty of failures and setbacks. They forged on to see the illuminating light of opportunity. They searched and found a better lifestyle, because of the liberties and freedom of positive thought, while adding a realistic pursuit for transformation, success, and happiness. Imagine you doing the same.

These are the same people who decided to become winners in spite of anything! They were F.E.A.R. LESS. They all had a transformational awakening breakthrough. They became invested in the idea that the achievement of "that special something" can be possible to those who really believe, have faith, take action and be persistent. They began to believe and create a mental, physical, emotional and financial path filled with direction for themselves as well as their families. They decided that winners never quit, and quitters never win.

By *"Finding Your Moment of Clarity,"* you can also discover the secret keys for your success, that are dormant and hidden within the energy of your own thoughts. You can discover that if you think that you can succeed, then you can. If you think that you can't, then you can't succeed! You no longer will buy into the idea that growing up on the wrong side of the tracks is a reason for permanent lifelong failure.

You will find out that when the dream is big enough, the facts don't count! You will discover that not if, but when you change your thoughts, you will change your present state of existence. Most importantly, like millions before you, you will realize that acts without faith, dreams without goals, and without taking action, and without having a vision, there will never be any kind of real success! Stay away from fantasy thinking and work your reality plan!

Think about and imagine you are now blazing your own trail for success. You have learned to accept the bumps, bruises, trials, tribulations, roadblocks, dead ends, setbacks, and even failure from time to time. Imagine you have learned to always pick yourselves up, dust yourselves off and keep on pushing. Think about and imagine pulling yourself up by your bootstraps. See yourself in your thoughts and mind, forging on until you experience the accomplishment of obtaining "that special something" that is currently, just a touch away from your fingertips of success. Become F.E.A.R. LESS!

Here are ten examples that I have embedded in my life's journey toward success. I refer to them regularly. I may not recite all ten every day. However, I read from this list out loud for my ears to hear.

READ ALOUD AS YOU COMPLETE THIS LIST

1. I will use the Universal power of my mind to consciously and deliberately shift how I think, feel and act, directly in comparison to my goals, dreams, and vision.

2. I will write down every single idea, and goal that comes to mind.

3. I will use the speed of implementation and start going after my idea, as soon as it comes to mind.

4. I will not be a wondering generality in life, I will be a meaningful specific by attaching a date of accomplishment to every one of my written goals.

5. I will use time management strategies to help keep me on track hourly, daily, weekly, monthly, quarterly, and yearly as my measuring stick for progress and accomplishment.

6. I will accept failure as a temporary lane change in the pursuit of "that special something" that I define as my goal, dream, and vision.

7. I will be coachable under the tutelage of a highly experienced person or persons who have the expertise that I need to achieve "that special something."

8. Two definitions of F.E.A.R., to contemplate are: Feeling Excited And Ready, and False Evidence Appearing Real.

9. I will not compare my success with others. However, I will stay in the race in the game of life and never give up or quit on my goals, dream, and most importantly, my vision.

10. I will lead by example; I will express my gratitude for every measure of success no matter how big or small. I will be of service to others while walking the walk, because the time is NOW, not someday, or tomorrow, NOW!

Were you born to WIN? Answering this question correctly will deliver the *"Finding Your Moment of Clarity" vision* needed for transformation, direction, enthusiasm, and most importantly, confirmation that you were indeed born to WIN. The next question is; DO YOU BELIEVE THAT YOU WERE BORN TO WIN?

CHAPTER 17
WHY I WAS BORN TO WIN EXERCISE

On a separate note pad or below, write down your top 5 reasons that you believe WHY you were born to win and WHY you will win!

1. _____

2. _____

3. _____

4. _____

5. _____

Remember; this is your WHY you were born to win and WHY you will win list, and yours alone. If you are married or if you are in a relationship, both participants should write out their own separate WHY list. It's ok to share your WHY list with your spouse or partner, however your list should come from your own thoughts.

It has been said that "Men are from Mars and Women are from Venus!" Having separate individual goals, dreams and visions is alright. In this case, the art of love, togetherness, support, and making WHY a team effort is important. Both partners will fully know that neither one of you are in competition with the other. You both will be stronger with the "all for one and one for all" Universal principle of oneness toward achievement of your WHY's. An essential factor is 100% honesty.

Begin today, to put into practice the necessary action steps needed that's equal to every reason that you stated as to WHY you were born to win.

WE BECOME WHO AND WHAT
WE THINK ABOUT

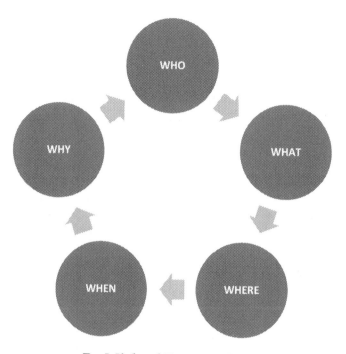

By Michael Bart Mathews

*Napoleon Hill – "Whatever the mind can
conceive and believe, it can achieve." The Mind is
Everything-What you think, you become."*

I magine going to bed at night for years, after thinking
about becoming the person that you want to become in
life. After waking up one morning, you discover that you
have actually transformed yourself and your life into those
thoughts, that are now your reality. As you humbly look back

and acknowledge your achievements, you also realize that your mindset was exactly the same today, as it was years ago, while you were thinking things that you consistently thought about over the past years.

Your thinking, your thoughts, and your actions all lead you to the exact place where you are in life today. Are you happy with your current lot in life? Are your past thoughts, equal to the current lifestyle that you are living today? Do you believe that if you change your thoughts, you will change your life?

Up to this point, you read about; how the power of your own thoughts can change your life. How redefining F.E.A.R. and knowing that you can WIN, is more than just a possibility. You can shed the heavy emotional baggage blockers that have been weighing you down while standing in your way of achievement.

Without the 800-pound gorilla, called emotional baggage blockers, resting on your shoulders of transformation, the next question is, who or what do you want to become in life? What values do you want to embody? What self-improvements methods do you need to incorporate into your new life?

Going from being a wondering generality to becoming a meaningful specific; will involve a vast amount of time THINKING about the person that you want to become. You can become who and what you think about.

If you don't know who you are, or what you want, how do you know what it will take to reach your destination in life? What ideas from thought can you list that you can manifest into a tangible, realistic project for achievement?

SOME EXAMPLES ARE:

- ➤ I will become a servant leader by setting up a 501c3 foundation and serve the needs of people during transitional periods in their lives
- ➤ I will become a better spouse or partner
- ➤ I will become debt free and financially secure
- ➤ I will learn how to create, sustain, and pass on wealth to the next generation
- ➤ I will improve my life using personal growth, development, and self-help techniques
- ➤ I will get coaching to help guide and hold me accountable
- ➤ I will become a better parent
- ➤ I will become a benefit and not a burden to my family and community
- ➤ I will become a happier person
- ➤ I will become a successful business owner
- ➤ I will become more educated and knowledgeable in my business
- ➤ I will embrace the best improvement starts with self-improvement

Complete the exercise below to help identify the person you want to become. You will need to set goals for each in order to accomplish the change. But complete your list until you can clearly become who it is that you want to be and obtain what it is that you want to achieve in life.

Unbeknownst to you, you most likely have listed your heart's burning desire on this page. If you must, expand the list. You can refer back to this list when completing the next exercise. Keep an open mind, because when your mind is open like a parachute, ideas will flow, where attention and energy goes!

What do you think about day-in-and-day-out? What transformational changes must you undertake to become that new person who you think about? Our thoughts are powerful enough to determine our actions and the way we behave. The way we act (optimistic or pessimistic) shapes our reality in either a good or a bad way.

Controlling our thoughts by controlling our mind, in the direction of who it is that we want to become, and what it is that we want to achieve is second to none.

CHAPTER 18
WHO WILL I BECOME EXERCISE?

On your note pad or below, write down your top 5 passions, values, traits, characteristics, and behaviors to describe the person you want to become.

Now rank the list in order of importance with number 1 being the most important. Now based upon your ranking order, focus on completing one at a time.

1. _____

2. _____

3. _____

4. _____

5. _____

FINDING YOUR HEART'S BURNING DESIRE

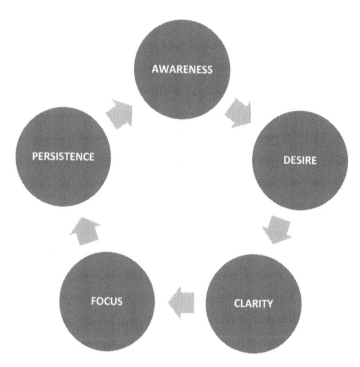

By Michael Bart Mathews

Y ou are now getting closer and closer to *"Finding Your Moment of Clarity"* in life if you have not done so already. Every contributing co-author has laid out multiple nuggets for your success. Please take full advantage of their guidance and coaching within the pages of their chapters.

We are all good at something special, displaying similar traits, gifts, and talents with others in some cases, and unlike no other, in other cases. Have you heard that if you can find your passion, then you can make it happen? When this occurs, you will never work a day in your life? Your work will become your play, and you can get paid for playing!

Imagine you took what you have been doing for years and years for free, and created a following of people who are willing to pay you for doing the same thing that you've always done.

What are some things that you currently enjoy doing, and are already extremely passionate about? Have you ever once thought about turning that passion into a home-based business? Have you thought about connecting with and partnering up with an existing startup or established business and offer your products and services in exchange for payment in the marketplace?

Take professional athletes for example; these are grown men and women who found their passion in life, early on in most cases. As a very young child, they played football, basketball, baseball, tennis, ran track or maybe boxing because they enjoyed doing it. As they got better and better, they became more and more passionate about competing. Because of their skills, passion, growth and personal development, they were able to identify their heart's burning desire. As adults in the professional ranks, they are getting paid multi-million-dollar contracts to do the very thing that they did for fun and for free as a child.

What are you doing now as a hobby because of your passion, that you can transform into a client-based business? Your current hobby or passion can become your heart's burning desire?

EXAMPLES OF THINGS YOU MIGHT ALREADY ENJOY DOING AND ARE PASSIONATE ABOUT:

➤ Sewing
➤ Conflict resolution/problem solving with your family and friends
➤ Providing information/the how-to, go to person
➤ Singing
➤ Writing
➤ Playing an instrument
➤ Teaching
➤ Training
➤ Consulting
➤ Cooking
➤ Interior home design
➤ Landscaping
➤ Handyman or Handy-Ann
➤ Numbers cruncher/bean counter (accountant)
➤ Speaking
➤ Planning/hosting
➤ Babysitting/Child Care
➤ Coaching (business, sports, life)

Complete the exercise below. Now look closely at your list. Rank them in order of the one you enjoy doing the most and are most passionate about. Using number one as the most enjoyable and passionate, and number five as being the least enjoyable or least passionate. Anyone of them has the potential and possibility to become your heart's burning desire!

This is a good time for you to dig deep down inside of your mind; reach out, dream big and believe in yourself. If you need to take a few moments and sit in a quiet place where the Universal energy of thought is at its highest reachable magnetic pulling point, in silence with no interruptions, then, by all means, take this moment in time to meditate on this subject.

When you find your heart's burning desire in life, you will have found the goose that lays the golden eggs. You will have found "Your Moment of Clarity."

CHAPTER 19
YOUR HEART'S BURNING DESIRE EXERCISE

On your note pad or below, write down your top 5 things that you are currently doing for free that you are most passionate about and enjoy doing. Things that give you joy and pleasure.

Now rank the list in order of importance with number 1 being the most important. Now based upon your ranking order, ask this question: "Can I turn this passion into profit?" If the answer is "No," move it down on the list until you get a "Yes." Focus on setting goals to turn your passion into profit!

1. _____

2. _____

3. _____

4. _____

5. _____

Note: If your passion involves helping people through volunteering, then don't remove it from the list. You will need to balance work (i.e. making money), family and service to ensure you can accomplish all of your heart's burning desires.

SECTION TWO

Finding Your Moment of Clarity Your Journey to Self-Improvement

TAKING ACTION – SET S.M.A.R.T. GOALS

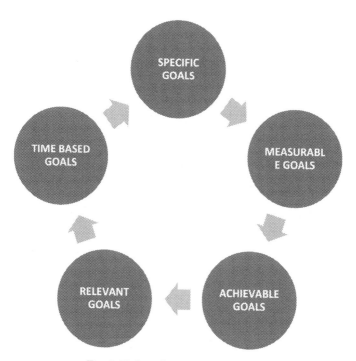

By Michael Bart Mathews

N ow that you removed the emotional baggage blockers that once held you back, you have defined the person you want to become. You have discovered your heart's burning desire, your WHY [reason or purpose-goal or dream]. You have formulated your think tank or mastermind group, compiled with like-minded people. It's now time to set some S.M.A.R.T goals and take action.

Merriam-Webster's definition of a goal states "Something that you are trying to do or achieve." That something is your WHY [reason or purpose - goal or dream]. That something is the motivating factor for setting S.M.A.R.T. goals in the first place. You have identified, without question, what "that special something" is you want to accomplish, so you can begin the S.M.A.R.T. goal setting process!

> "Success is the sum of all the choices you have made in your life. Everything in life happens because you took action. If it hasn't yet, it's because you didn't take enough action."
> -JT Foxx

Knowing what you want to accomplish is imperative in using speed and implementation of action if you're going to achieve it.

Goal setting is the standard choice of highly successful people, while others set no goals at all. The question is, if you don't know where you are going, how will you know when you get there? Go back and re-read about the growth cycle of the Chinese bamboo tree before you undertake this exercise.

An American philosopher named Elbert Hubbard understood that many people failed in their endeavors. He also said that "people failed not because they lacked intelligence or courage, but because they did not organize their energies around a goal."

A survey talks about goal setting with Harvard MBA students.

Question: why do 3% of Harvard MBA's make ten times as much as the other 97%?

Answer: They set clear, written goals for their future and made plans to accomplish them. You don't have to be a Harvard MBA to understand the importance of setting goals. As simple as goal setting may sound, the lack of achievement comes from little or no goal setting habits by millions, upon millions of people. Our chances of achieving success at a higher level are associated with setting goals.

S.M.A.R.T. goals are a system that helps you create and use to achieve the accomplishments that you seek while developing transformational, results-driven habits for personal growth, development, and success. Like the most successful people on the planet from past to present, we can also benefit from adopting and setting S.M.A.R.T. goals effectively.

LET'S GO OVER THE FIVE-PART S.M.A.R.T. GOAL SYSTEM:

1. **SPECIFIC** (clearly defined or identified).

Specific goals must be crystal clear and clearly defined. If you don't know where you're going, how will you know which road to take? Being a meaningful specific from the start will save you the setback of experiencing being a wandering generality. Having vague or generalized goals is like the space shuttle having no rocket boosters powerful enough to lift it off from the launching pad and propel it, up and out of the gravitational pull of earth's atmosphere. The goal is to lift the spacecraft off the launching pad, but without rocket boosters, it's not going to happen. Having specific goals is equivalent to having your very own rocket boosters that will lift you off your launching pad toward success!

2. **MEASURABLE** (able to be measured).

Measurable goals must include before, during, and most importantly, after results. Begin with the end in mind. By being specific from the start, you can measure your progress along your journey. Having measurable goals is like baking a delicious German Chocolate cake from scratch. Some of the measurable goals in baking that cake consists of different ingredients like; baking chocolate, water, baking soda, salt, granulated sugar, butter, eggs, vanilla, buttermilk, chopped pecans, and walnuts. Before adding each ingredient, each much be measured. Like adding each measurable ingredient while baking a cake, you add more measurable tasks (ingredients) toward achieving success.

3. **ACHIEVABLE** (realistic-attainable and able to be reached successfully).

Obtaining achievable goals is like trying to eat a whole elephant. Eating a whole elephant at one sitting is not possible. However, eating it one bite at a time, over time is possible. Beginning with the end in mind will give you the necessary small bite size goals that should not be so insurmountable or out of reach. With each smaller bite-size goal that you achieve, find a way to give yourself a small reward for accomplishment. Don't break the piggy bank, however, with each goal that you complete along your journey, continued action will give you the much need faith to persist. Remember, success, like eating an elephant is one bite at a time!

4. **RELEVANT** (closely connected or appropriate to what is being done or considered).

Relevant goals should always perfectly align directly with your action plan for success. Being consistent with your actions will develop proper habits that are specifically directed toward obtaining that specific special something that you seek. If your end goal is to become a pediatrician, don't include a goal in your action plan to climb Mount Everest. It is not required or relevant to become a pediatrician. However, after achieving becoming a pediatrician, you can plan to climb Mount Everest if you so desire!

5. **TIME BOUND** (a goal that is measured or restricted by time).

Time-bound goals prevent you from becoming a wondering generality with no end result or destination in plain sight. If you plan to travel to Dubai, the duration of your flight will take around 13 hours and 20 minutes of flight time from Chicago's O'Hare International Airport. If your goal is to travel from Chicago to St. Louis by automobile, it takes approximately 4 hours and 16 minutes (depending on what part of Chicago you depart from). Like flying to Dubai or driving to St. Louis, your personal and business goals all should have a starting route, or plan and ending point. It should also have a completion date. Always begin with the end in mind!

Here are some examples of S.M.A.R.T. and not so SMART goals:

➤ **Not a SMART goal:** "I want to lose weight."
➤ **SMART goal:** "I want to lose 50 pounds by May 30, 2019. I will perform 30 minutes of cardio and 30 minutes of strength training per day, 6 times a week. I will only eat carbohydrates 2 times a week and fresh fruit and vegetables 7 days per week."

➤ **Not a SMART goal:** "I want to write a book."
➤ **SMART goal:** "I want to write a book" that is at least 200 pages in length and complete it by August 30, 2019. I will write at least 6.6 pages for thirty days straight, and my book will be completed in one month. Or I will write 3.3 pages every day for two months, and my book will be completed in 60 days.

Now you can begin the S.M.A.R.T. goal setting process for your heart's burning desire, your WHY [reason or purpose-goal or dream]. Your goals can be short-term, medium-term and or long-term. You can define the periods for each of these terms. But always begin with the end in mind. For example, if you set a goal to be completed in 12 months, set goals/tasks/actions for each month, week and day to ensure you can accomplish your goals one bite at a time.

Here are some examples of short, medium, and long-term goals. The key is to be as specific as you can from start to achievement:

SHORT TERM GOALS USUALLY ARE FOR A PERIOD OF ONE TO FIVE MONTHS:

- ➤ I will start the paperwork for my business entity on March 1st.
- ➤ I will read one book every month starting March 1st.
- ➤ I will pay my bills on time every month starting March 1st.
- ➤ I will save $500 every month starting March 1st.
- ➤ I will start debt reduction/elimination rollover payment plan on March 1st.

MEDIUM TERM GOALS ARE USUALLY SIX MONTHS TO ONE YEAR:

- ➤ I will take my heart's burning desire and turn it into a for-profit business by December 31st, 2019.
- ➤ I will take a trip to an exotic, tropical location in Costa Rica one year from now.
- ➤ I will save $100 per month for one year to pay the total cost of my trip.
- ➤ I will slowly purchase with cash the things I will need for my trip over the next twelve months.
- ➤ I will work on my craft until I master it starting March 1st.
- ➤ I will invest $25,000 in my business education starting March 1st for twelve months.

LONG TERM GOALS ARE USUALLY BETWEEN FIVE AND TEN PLUS YEARS:

- ➤ I will research and develop my products and services, making them available for sale in the global marketplace within 24 months starting March 1st.
- ➤ In five years, I will be completely out of debt. I will start my plan on March 1st.
- ➤ In ten years, I will be financially stable and ready for retirement. I will increase my retirement savings by 25% starting March 1st until I retire.
- ➤ In seven years, I will sell my home and become a world traveler, living in 5 different countries with no time limit or restrictions.
- ➤ I will have multiple streams of passive income starting January 1st.

MANY FAMOUS AND SUCCESSFUL MEN AND WOMEN BELIEVE IN THE POWER OF SETTING GOALS:

- ➤ *Napoleon Hill – "The world has the habit of making room for the man (woman) whose actions show that he (she) knows where he (she) is going."*
- ➤ *Oprah Winfrey – "If you want to accomplish the goals of your life, you have to begin with the spirit."*
- ➤ *Zig Ziglar – "What you get by achieving your goals is not as important as what you become by achieving your goals."*
- ➤ *Earl Nightingale – "People with goals succeed because they know where they're going."*
- ➤ *Lisa Nichols - "When your clarity meets your conviction, and you apply action to the equation, your world will begin to transform before your eyes."*
- ➤ *Benjamin E. Mays – "It must be borne in mind that the tragedy of life doesn't lie in not reaching your goal. The tragedy lies in having no goals to reach."*

As you can see, S.M.A.R.T. GOALS can be used by anyone, at any time, to achieve almost anything. You don't need any special skills or tools, and you don't need to be a Harvard MBA. However, you must grind it out while sticking to your goals in order for this process to yield the necessary results that you seek. No risk, no action, no reward.

S.M.A.R.T. GOALS will work if you work them. S.M.A.R.T. GOALS will not work if you do not work them. Developing the habit of staying focused on the end result is a must. If you want "that specific special something" bad enough, S.M.A.R.T. GOALS will shine a brighter light and illuminate your path as you walk your journey.

CHAPTER 20
S.M.A.R.T. GOALS EXERCISE

On your note pad, write down your top 5 short, medium, or long-term NOT SMART goals based upon your WHY, reason, purpose, goal or dream. OK, I know this doesn't make sense based upon what I said above-LOL. However, just getting a quick list of goals you want to accomplish written down will allow you to turn them into S.M.A.R.T. goals below.

1. _____

2. _____

3. _____

4. _____

5. _____

So, that you can begin to take action, now turn the NOT SMART goals above into S.M.A.R.T goals. Refer back to the above examples if necessary. Or visit our website www. tmeinc.com and download our Live W.E.A.L.T.H.Y. – S.M.A.R.T. Goals Template.

1. _____

2. _____

3. _____

4. _____

5. _____

Remember, a goal without an action plan is like a ship without strong winds blowing its sails or fuel for its engine. You will float aimlessly. You must be specific, and you must take action!

BUILDING RELATIONSHIP CAPITAL

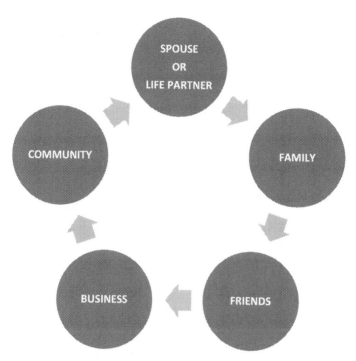

By Michael Bart Mathews

First, let me share a quick, true powerful story with you. In March of 2018, I was standing in the lobby of my Hollywood hotel waiting on a taxi to take me to attend the City Summit/Gala. Out of nowhere appeared a well dress man, who was very vibrant and full of energy, and most importantly, he was exceptionally friendly. He spoke with a New York accent, and he was carrying a white box. The stranger asked me; "hey, are you going to the City Summit/ Gala? And are you waiting for a taxi?" I smiled and said, "yes, you might as well ride with me." The stranger said, "hi I'm Brandon." "I said hello, I'm Michael."

Then Brandon went on to say; "hey, you look like a baller (basketball player)." I told him that I played back in the day. He asked me who did I play with? I said that I played with some of the best of the best high school, College, European, and American professional basketball players during my time. I did give him several names. However, I won't mention them here. Before I could say another word, Brandon began telling me about a 3 on 3 basketball game he played against a player who happened to have played for the Chicago Bulls and has six championship rings. Yes, you already know who he was talking about!

We got into the taxi, and Brandon began telling me about when he was young, and he had a paper route, and how he figured out a way to become successful selling newspapers (after failing in the beginning). Brandon told me that his mother asked him, what else can he do for his customers that would help him to build and grow. He said to me that along with delivering his newspapers, he also delivered his customers' fresh milk and bagels. His 5th-grade business grew because he offered more value than any other paper boys in his neighborhood.

Before we exited the taxi, Brandon asked me for my business card. We said departing pleasantries as we both entered the City Summit/Gala, while quickly getting separated in the large crowd of attendees. About two hours later, while sitting in the audience; the Master of Ceremony introduced the next speaker. I noticed the next speaker was the stranger (now known to me as Brandon) who rode with me in the taxi and asked me for my business card earlier that day.

Ladies and Gentlemen, our next speaker, is Brandon Steiner; CEO of Steiner Sports, the leading producer of authentic hand-signed collectibles and sports memorabilia in all of North

America. He also bought Yankee Stadium among many other business ventures.

As Brandon Steiner was speaking; I said to myself "he probably did play and win that 3 on 3 basketball game against that professional basketball player who has six championships rings." I say this because those of you who do not know Brandon Steiner, might ask yourself, can he play the game, let alone imagining who he played against.

Several days after I returned home from the event, I received an email from Brandon Steiner's personal assistant requesting my address. The email stated that Mr. Steiner said it was a pleasure meeting you and he wants to send you a gift. I responded in kind, as well as giving my address. Then I forgot all about it because of being busy. About one week after receiving the email, I received a white box in the mail. It was the exact same kind of white box that Brandon Steiner was carrying when I first met him on the way to the City Summit/Gala. I opened the box and inside were three gifts.

1. A copy of his book titled *You Gotta Have Balls*.
2. A Steiner Sports Pen with dirt from Yankee Stadium-with a Certificate of Authenticity.
3. A major league baseball with the following one-liners inscribed on it:
   - It's not the game, it's the plan
   - What's your value proposition
   - The grass is not greener on the other side, it green where you water it
   - What's winning for you
   - If it's easy, it isn't possible
   - Commitment leads to passion
   - 1st 90 seconds of your day

My point for sharing my story with you is to show you how important each and every single person that you meet can be, even when you least expect it. Brandon Steiner took the opportunity to add value to my life. True, not everyone will add value, unlike my story, however, you will never know who will if you don't understand how important it is to build relationship capital with everyone that you cross paths with.

As you begin your new-found journey toward success, you will need to build new relationships along the way. You will lose some old friends and possibly family as you fulfill your dreams. But you will find new like-minded people to inspire you along the way.

Imagine if I would have prejudged Brand Steiner and displayed negative energy. Do you think for a moment that he would have shared two of his many experiences with me (the total stranger at that time), as well as have his personal assistant email me, then send me the three gifts?

The moral and lesson that Brandon Steiner imparted in me were the following five nuggets:

1. Don't prejudge people.
2. Be friendly.
3. Display positive energy.
4. Offer a value proposition in some way.
5. Be memorable because you were fun to be around.

Re-read Brandon Steiner's five nuggets that I mentioned above. How can you apply them into your everyday thought process? Imagine adopting building relationship capital with everyone you meet without first prejudging them. Imagine how fast your database of new people will organically grow by leaps and bounds.

Imagine you looked and dressed like Jed Clampett on the Beverly Hillbillies (the once impoverished mountaineer/now millionaire unbeknownst to the store merchant) and you were on a shopping spree in downtown Beverly Hills. Imagine you not pulling up in your Benz, BMW, Bentley or Rolls Royce.

Instead like Jed, you pulled up in your old beater of a vehicle and parked directly in front of the high-end stores.

Think about how many merchants, upon first seeing people who dressed like Jed, prejudged him (you) and his (your) intentions while turning their nose up speculating Jed (you) cannot afford to purchase anything in the store just because of outward appearance. Now Mr. Drysdale (the local banker) walks in the store and actually calls Jed by his name. As a matter of fact, he calls Jed; "Mr. Clampett!"

Now the merchant has a different opinion of Jed because of the friendly, and publicly pleasing relationship capital Jed has with Mr. Drysdale (the banker). The store merchant made a 360-degree relationship capital, paradigm shift by adjusting his attitude. He began to treat Jed just like he could afford to purchase anything in the store.

How many Jed Clampett looking people have you unknowingly dismissed because of their outward appearance? If you are in a prosperous financial position in life, while you were shopping and dressed down, how many times has this happen to you? If you are not in a good financial place in life, how many times has this happened to you?

My point is that there is a ton of room for building relationship capital with everyone. The old saying goes; never judge a book by its cover. Well never judge the success of a person when they are not dressed appropriately for the situation or event.

Just like my above two examples. One factual (Brandon Steiner) and one fictional (Jed Clampett), how well you get along in harmony and good spirits with others is always important. Some people display an openly pleasing personality, pleasant attitude, more often than not, they are happy, spirited people. They are very approachable and make friends easily. They are the life of the party, so to speak!

How well you introspectively get along with yourself (your thoughts-the inner you, that inner voice) is a determining factor about how harmoniously you get along with others. Showoffs and people who brown nose tend to display artificial emotions and personalities in order to be accepted into the in-crowd or be in good grace with others.

By being your authentic natural self with the relationships you have with others, you will display precisely who you are. By nature, you should always want to be seen as being authentic and genuine in the eyes of others. You won't need to show off or brown nose to gain likeability or acceptance. Some people will like you some of the time, while others will dislike you at other times. Remember you can fool some of the people some of the time, however, you can't fool all of the people, all of the time. Be yourself and let the chips fall where they may. You will never need to hide behind a fake mask. The oil will rise to the top of the water, and you will develop positive, rock solid, like-minded relationships.

As one of my coaches, *Dr. James Dentley often says: "Some people will be a good memory while others will be a terrible reminder!" Which memory will you be to others?*

I get along harmoniously well in the following relationships, circle the correct answers below:

Myself	Yes	No	
Spouse	Yes	No	
Children	Yes	No	
Authority	Yes	No	
Boss	Yes	No	
Friends	Yes	No	
Strangers	Yes	No	
Co-workers	Yes	No	

"A RELATIONSHIP is not based on the length of time you've spent together. It's based on the FOUNDATION you've built together. Build your relationships deep, and build them strong, in order for the roots to withstand the test of time."
-Michael Bart Mathews

If you answered no to any of the above, ask yourself what changes can be made to improve those relationships? There is a thin thread in life, one minute we are here and the next minute we're gone! While you are in good health and of sound mind, make every attempt to right any wrongs that are like a plague that is destroying that relationship. If the relationship is worth salvaging, who is right, and who is wrong does not matter. At least make an attempt (offer an olive branch) to right any wrongs while you have the opportunity to do so! Then move on!

Think about the person or people who (for whatever reason) you no longer see eye-to-eye with? That person might be one of your family members, an old friend, a neighbor, or someone from the list above. Think about all the good times, the fun, the laughter, the precious memories you shared together before stinking thinking set in?

Imagine you being the bigger person and you make the phone call or knock on the door of forgiveness and simply say some kind, encouraging, inspirational words of peace and harmony. Imagine you are extending your hand while greeting that person. Now think about seeing that person flash a big smile of acceptance and approval. Now imagine that dark cloud that has drenched your past relationship with stinking thinking has suddenly turned into the bright, shining, illuminating light filled with new faith, hope, and forgiveness.

Imagine having a warm embrace of acceptance because you were the bigger person who stepped up to the plate of righteousness and passed the olive branch. Imagine tears of joy streaming down from your eyes because you have repaired the stinkin thinking that caused the problems between you both stemming from your past troubles.

Imagine you actually saying that you are sorry for your part and you apologize for whatever part you contributed into the dismantling of your once vibrant relationship. Imagine you have put your pride to the side, and you took the first step toward righting the wrong that has kept you apart from your once beloved, good, and healthy relationship.

Keep in mind that we also outgrow relationships. If someone on your list is unwilling to accept your olive branch, going forward, stay in your lane and forge on with the healthy relationships that you have in your life. Learn how to accept the things that you cannot change, and the courage to change the things that you can.

CHAPTER 21
BUILDING RELATIONSHIPS EXERCISE

On your note pad or below, write down at least 5 people that you will make an attempt to get along with more harmoniously. Do not stop until you have rebuilt positive relationship capital with at least one person on your list.

1. _____

2. _____

3. _____

4. _____

5. _____

Also write down, at least 5 new relationships sources that you will pursue. For example, I will join the local chamber of commerce, BNI group, attend meetups, conferences, and seminars to meet other local business owners. I will join an organization at a school that shares my interests.

1. _____

2. _____

3. _____

4. _____

5. _____

MASTERMIND TIME

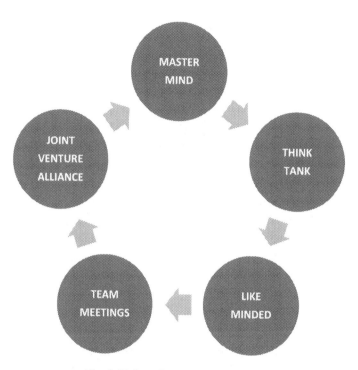

By Michael Bart Mathews

N ow that you have discovered your heart's burning desire, it's time to reach out to other like-minded people who understand how you think, act and feel about making it happen. As you will realize, when you are driving down the road to success, you will run into three types of people along the way. This is where soul searching, and personal development will make the rubber meet the road, and really comes into play.

1. **HATERS;** either don't want you to succeed, or they don't mind if you succeed, as long as you don't pass

them up! This is a mentally toxic group, and it is in your best interest to stay as far away from them as possible. In the beginning, they say things like, "who do you think you are" "what makes you think you can do that?" If you fail, and give up or quit, they will be the first in line to say, "I knew you couldn't do it."

2. **CONGRATULATORS**; they are 100% genuinely happy for the mere fact that you choose not to flock with the sheep of disparity. That you think outside of the box, or that you just threw the box away. They are happy that you have a goal, you have a dream, you have found your heart's burning desire that is the fuel for your fire called accomplishment and success.

3. **SIDELINE VIEWERS**; they are people who always think inside of the box. They do the same thing day in and day out. They always complain, but never try to improve their circumstances. They are conformist, still putting up with the status quo! They don't hate you, they don't congratulate you, but they will, from time to time check in and see what progress, or lack of progress you are making. Depending on your success or failure, determines if they turn into congratulators or haters!

When selecting your think tank or mastermind group, be very selective. This group will expedite your personal growth and development and should consist of people who are more successful than you. People who have already blazed the trail that you are getting ready to follow. People who in some way, directly specializes and has already gone, or is currently going in the same direction as you. People who can teach you tricks of the trade, while you are learning the ropes. Most importantly, they all should have a like-minded, positive mental attitude about themselves first and foremost.

If you are always the smartest person in your group, you need to find another group! You can stunt your personal growth if the people you are constantly around can't share with you new, innovative and creative concepts.

And just because a person is successful, that doesn't always mean that he or she is the right person for your team. They may be an excellent thought leader, coach or mentor. However, they might display the "I'm the King or Queen of the Hill attitude." This type of person wants to hold court and is always openly braggadocios about their accomplishments, instead of having the attitude of gratitude, being thankful, humble and down to earth. So, give the people who you are considering asking to become a member of your think tank or mastermind group some serious thought.

Complete the exercise below to find a list of potential candidates. Follow them while doing your due diligence along the way. Learn from them. Attend their masterminds, conferences, seminars or other events. This will help you to know how they think and operate to determine if they are a good fit for what you are seeking to receive or share.

This will assist you in expanding out of your comfort zone, while building new valuable relationships, with like-minded people, along your journey. Yes; there may be an occasional investment involved if you want to change some things in your life. Investments yield ROI's known as return on investment. Don't look at it as a cost.

Expand your list of names until you reached the desired number of leaders. Try and have an odd number in case of a vote which needs a tiebreaker. The direction, ideas, and thoughts from others will allow you to learn and grow, from the many different experiences and strategies that you alone, might not have ever thought about. You will have more sources of positive energy from thought to draw upon!

Like every co-author within the pages of this book. We all teamed up and put our thoughts in writing and formed a mastermind/think tank group, for your personal reading pleasure.

CHAPTER 22
MASTERMIND TIME EXERCISE

On your note pad or below, write down your list of at least 5 people who you want to participate in your think tank or mastermind group discussions. If you can't think of anyone, research (e.g., Google, Facebook groups, LinkedIn and other platforms) people that are doing the things that you want to do.

1. _____

2. _____

3. _____

4. _____

5. _____

CHAPTER 23

ACCOUNTABILITY COACHING

By Michael Bart Mathews

O ne of the best gifts you can give yourself is the gift of Coaching. Success leaves clues! Having a good coach in the game of life gives you a seasoned pair of eyes and ears to help you win in the game of life. Coaching will allow you to draw your X's & O's. Your coach will guide you through each play by play, success driven, action-based offense that champions are made from. When it's time to play defense or say no, your coach will be there. You cannot win every game, and you cannot close every business deal. However, having a coach can lead to more victories than defeats.

Coaching is a creative and collaborative process. This process is about you coming to the realization that you can discover change and succeed in your personal and business life beyond your current thinking. Coaching has very profound effects on who wins, and who loses in sports as well as in the game of life. By controlling your mind using the power of positive thinking, and accountability results coaching, you will be well on your way to accomplishment.

Most of the greatest world leaders from past to present, in the political arena, in the corporate world, in the private sector, and in the wide world of sports, have consistently used or are using accountability results coaching to help them stay focused on the action plan for success.

As a former basketball player, for our team to have won several different championships, looking as far back as high school, our leaders were actually our accountability results coaches.

In High School, my team won the 1973 Class AA Chicago City and Illinois State High School Basketball Championship titles. During the summer of 1973, my (CNBL) Chicago Neighborhood Basketball League Team won the Chicago City Title and the National Title in Baltimore Maryland.

In college, my teams reached four consecutive (I participated in two) postseason NAIA-National Association of Intercollegiate Athletics tournaments. All my high school and college wins were a result of good coaching.

While playing in the Chicago summer PRO/AM tournaments in the late '70s & early '80s with and against some of best college, European and NBA players during my time, we had excellent coaching. I'll name a few of the players starting with; Wallace" Mickey" Johnson, Rickey Green, Sonny Parker, Maurice "Bo" Ellis, Maurice "Mo" Cheeks, Flynn Robinson, Jeff Wilkins, Stevie King, Lonnie Lewis, and many others.

They all used their professional experience during game situations, as well as during timeouts. Guess what, they all were player-coaches.

I had the luxury of playing with Rickey Green in high school. He was the floor general (player-coach) while our bench coach Charles Stimpson ran the X's and O's. Those, early in my life, coaching experiences allowed me to understand the importance of coaching in sports. It correlates to the personal and business X's and O's in the game of life today!

Today, I use the same basketball related winning principals in the game of life. However, I have multiple business and personal accountability results coaches. They are here to tell me what I need to hear, not what I may want to hear!

You don't have to be an athlete to learn how to play in the game of life! However, by utilizing the experience of a good coach, the game of life might not be so insurmountable that you can't win while playing at a higher level. Your coach will design your key plays for success based on your truthfulness from the information that you discuss together. Now you will be ready to play full out in the game of life.

Your coach will hold you accountable in the game of life similar to the X's and O's of any sport. The only difference is, in sports, the game last until the final second ticks off the scoreboard. In the game of life, you live it day in and day out. There is no time out, only until you leave this earth in a pine box. The game of life lives and plays on for as long as you live! And if you play the game right, your positive impact can live on from one generation to the next!

It is for you to determine what changes you want to make, and when you want to start making those changes. This creative, collaborative process reveals how you currently think, act and feel based upon your present thoughts, feelings, and actions.

This creative, collaborative process is about helping you to take control of your future by changing some things in the present, so you won't keep repeating mistakes from the past, with the assistance of your accountability coach. It's about you re-programming your mind and getting rid of the destructive, emotional baggage blockers that stand in the way of you being the best you, that you can become. This book is about helping you while you are *"Finding Your Moment of Clarity"* using the magical power of positive thought and accountability results coaching.

This creative, collaborative process is about helping you to introduce yourself to the new you. The innovative thinker, the inspired believer, the motivated goal setter, the new transformational go-getter and action taker. It's about helping you to open up your mind like a parachute in flight, gliding under the natural power of positive thought energy from the wind current, headed for the transformational change within the direction of your choosing.

This creative, collaborative process is about helping you to understand that you do have the power to create a new, vibrant, positive, successful, fulfilling, happy life. As long as you decide that this is the life that you want to establish for yourself and your family. The coach can take a person to the well, but they can't make them drink the water! How thirsty are you to change your thoughts so you can transform your life? It all depends on how positive you are now, in the present, and how you think, act and feel about life, liberty and the pursuit of happiness.

> *"It never cease to amaze me at the power of the coaching process to draw out the skills or talent that was previously hidden within an individual, and which invariably finds a way to solve a problem previously thought unsolvable."*
> *-John Russell*

Jessie Owens, against all the odds, went to Berlin Germany in 1936 and became the first American track and field athlete to win four gold medals in a single Olympiad. Usain Bolt (as of 2016) won nine gold medals. Steffi Graf (as of 2017) won twenty-two Grand Slam Tennis Titles with Serena Williams winning twenty-three. Bill Russell won eleven NBA Championships, Henri Richard won eleven Stanley Cup Championships with the Montreal Canadians, Martina Navratilova won nine Wimbledon's and four US Open titles.

What did each athlete have in common? It was, "coaching." And you can too! Along with good coaching and peak physical fitness, each person listed above had to possess the power of positive thinking, the magic of thinking big and the magic of believing they could WIN.

By enlisting the help of a coach, you can also WIN in the game of life. You will benefit from their personal and professional expertise and experience. When you succeed, your coach will succeed, and not before. Let's make no mistake, even with an accountability results coach, you must grind it out and do the work, bar none!

There are countless examples in your own life span of how an ordinary person, rose up and accomplished extraordinary things. Who were your elementary or high school friends who went on to achieve extraordinary things? Who rose up later in life to also accomplish extraordinary things? Ask them, who was their mentor or coach.

This creative, collaborative process can help better prepare you for the many opportunities that the Universe has to offer. Remember, if you think it, and you want it bad enough, use the positive power of thought and allow the person staring back at you in the glass mirror help you achieve it. Invest in yourself. Invest in accountability coaching!

NFL Head Football Coach Pete Carroll – "Each person holds so much power within themselves that needs to be let out. Sometimes they just need a little nudge, a little direction, a little support, a little coaching, and greatest things can happen."

Allow yourself to flow through the vortex, meaning letting the good stuff in. Remove those emotional baggage blockers that can stifle your positive vibrations and directions of thoughts, feelings, and actions. Align yourself to and with the positive source of energy that will allow you to feel and constantly experience enthusiasm, inspiration, motivation, passion, joy, gratefulness, gratitude, happiness, and appreciation for life and healthy relationships with yourself as well as with others. There is no greater joy, than joy itself! Your accountability results coach can help you achieve your hearts burning desire. If you really and truly want "that special something" that you most desire, two heads are better than one!

"Finding Your Moment of Clarity" by discovering your power within, as your mind leads you in the directions of your heart's desires, is as good as it gets. The mind is a cosmic wormhole, vessel or funnel of thought that has the ability to bring you into conscious awareness. An illuminating bright directional beacon of light and clarity, as you see life through your own eyes, as well as through the eyes of your coach!

The different frequencies and vibrations that manifest feelings of having a balanced lifestyle by way of you making certain choices. Letting the good stuff in or being in the vortex of life, liberty and the pursuit of happiness is available to everyone. It all depends on how you think, feel and act. We become what we think about. Control your thoughts, and you will control your life!

Let me end with two quotes from two of the many teachings that have and continues to help shape me to continually be in the vortex while allowing good things to enter and manifest in my life.

Ralph Waldo Emerson — "Do not go where the path may lead, go instead where there is no path and leave a trail."

Napoleon Hill — "Everything begins with an idea."

If you want a faster chance at rising to the top of that which you seek, explore hiring a coach. Find someone who you feel can tell you what you need to know, and not what you want to hear. I encourage you to research all of my special guest co-authors, as well as myself. Allow one or all of us to help take you off of the sideline of life! Allow one of us to help you achieve your desired results and success in that which you seek in the game of life. Allow us to help you discover "that special something" by assisting you in mind-mapping your X's & O's along your personal and or business journey in the game of life.

Let us walk hand in hand with you up to the free throw line, and cheer you on while you bend your knees, aim for the back of the rim, and hold it high and let it fly until you hear the swish from the ball going through the net. Now you have a better understanding of why personal and professional coaching is so important.

To view an excellent video depicting how important the gift of coaching can be in your life, watch this short YouTube video https://youtu.be/SF-G3fcFJgw. It's about the impact from one of the winningest coaches of all times, Coach John Wooden, had on his team and society. His *Pyramid of Success Coaching* strategy was one of the keys to his success and the success of those who followed his approach.

THE FIVE HOUR RULE

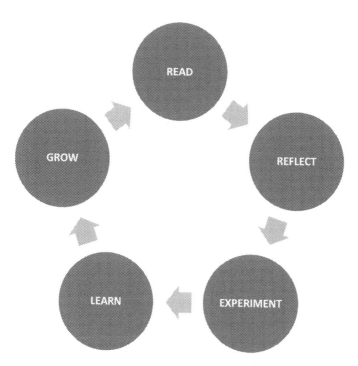

By Michael Bart Mathews

THE FIVE-HOUR RULE

N ow that your mind has been opened to endless possibilities, you must continuously fill it with the knowledge and wisdom needed to achieve your goals. There are numerous ways for you to learn and accomplish this. People learn best in different ways. You can apply one or more ways to acquire more knowledge along the way.

Mahatma Gandhi – "Live as if you were to die tomorrow. Learn as if you were to live forever."

Here are some of the different ways that people use for learning based on several research experiments from experts.

1. Visual (spatial) using pictures, images.
2. Aural (auditory) learning by sound.
3. Verbal (linguistic) words in speech and writing.
4. Physical (kinesthetic) using your body, hands, and touch.
5. Logical (mathematical) prefers using logic, reasoning, and systems.
6. Social (interpersonal) learns in groups or with other people.
7. Solitary (intrapersonal) alone in solitude and uses self-study.

However, studies have shown that the most successful people on this planet are also the people who are the likeliest to schedule and devote a minimum of at least one hour per day, for 5 days a week doing deliberate learning, reading and reflecting. Bill Gates, Warren Buffett, Mark Cuban, Oprah Winfrey, Elon Musk, Barak Obama and many other millionaires and billionaires attribute the art of reading and the art of continued learning as reasons for helping them to succeed at a higher level.

THE THREE PILLARS THAT MAKE UP THE FIVE HOUR RULE ARE:

1. **READING:** successful people at the highest levels read between one to three hours per day, if not more. You can gradually work your way into

"A mind that is stretched by a new experience can never go back to its old dimensions."
-Oliver Wendell Homes

your goal by at least starting to read anywhere from 15 to 30 minutes per day. Once you develop the habit of reading, start increasing your reading time by as little as 10-minute segments until you have reached the one-hour minimum.

Research has also stated that readers are leaders. It has also been suggested that reading personal growth and development/self-help books are the favorites of the wealthy. Some leaders read multiple books at a time. While others read one book at a time using speed-reading techniques to read faster. Learning to speed read will enable you to read more books in a short period of time.

Having a home library with physical books or stored on your electronic device is where a treasure trove of information, knowledge and wisdom will always be within arm's reach or at your fingertips. Your local library is also an excellent place to get lost in the literary world of reading. Do you have your library card? Below I will make a short list of books that peaked my attention and helped transform my mindset over time.

These books (and many more) have positively transformed and expanded my thinking in the areas of self-actualization, personal growth and development, thought leadership, personal finances, building relationship capital, organizational skills, the power of service to others, team building, and partnerships. They provide access to the wisdom from someone who has been there and done that. The acquisition and application of the knowledge you get from reading gives you the power to change your life, as you continue to grow while gaining knowledge.

Honestly, life is no game, however, once we learn how to play it, our work will be our play, and we will get paid to play. Once your mind has been stretched, it can never return back to its original form! While you are reading, open up your mind like a parachute descending from an airplane. Absorb every ounce of knowledge, like the parachute absorbs air to make a smooth landing. What books have you read, or are currently reading? I'm always seeking more transformational knowledge.

MY SHORT LIST OF BOOKS THAT HAVE CHANGED MY LIFE ARE, HOWEVER, NOT LIMITED TO:

1. *Think and Grow Rich – Napoleon Hill*
2. *Financially Speaking: The Best Improvement Starts with Self-Improvement – Michael Bart Mathews*
3. *The Magic of Thinking Big – David J. Schwartz*
4. *The Magic of Believing – Claude Bristol*
5. *The 7 Habits of Highly Effective People – Steven Covey*
6. *How to Win Friends and Influence People – Dale Carnegie*
7. *The Richest Man in Babylon – George S. Clason*
8. *Five Frequencies of Higher PERFORMANCE – James Dentley*
9. *Equanimity – Climbing Mount Entrepreneur – Dave Blanchard/Og Mandino Institute*
10. *The Observers Chair – Dave Blanchard/Og Mandino Institute*
11. *48 Laws of Power – Robert Greene*
12. *Acres of Diamonds – Russell Conwell*
13. *Rich Dad Poor Dad – Robert Kiyosaki*
14. *The Millionaire Next Door – Thomas J. Stanley*
15. *Millionaire Woman Next Door – Thomas J. Stanley*
16. *The Millionaires Club – Helen Cooper*
17. *Millionaire Underdog – JT Foxx*
18. *The Automatic Millionaire – David Bach*
19. *Do You Really Want to be an Entrepreneur – Karel Vermeulen*
20. *Bravest Journey – Amy Sayama*
21. *Your Greatest Potential!! Mastering Your Thinking, Create The Life You Desire – Natalie Bonomo*

John Wooden – "Five years from now, you're the same person except for the people you've met and the books you've read."

THE SECOND PILLAR OF THE FIVE-HOUR RULE IS:

2. **REFLECT:** reflecting or thinking (re-read The Art of Meditation) can be time well spent doing just that; reflecting and thinking. This is where new ideas, paradigm shifts, transformational a-ha moments come to mind while *Finding Your Moment of Clarity*. This is where Feeling Excited and Ready can begin to manifest within your present thoughts. Spend around fifteen minutes with pen and paper in hand to write down your ideas and any a-ha breakthrough, transformational ideas that suddenly appear. Thoughts of past setbacks or achievements, as well as future plans for transformation, may come to mind. Whatever your thought flow is, embrace it from an optimistic viewpoint, rather than from a pessimistic viewpoint.

THE THIRD PILLAR OF THE FIVE-HOUR RULE IS:

3. **EXPERIMENT:** apply learned knowledge to real-life situations or scenarios. A good example is the completion of this book that you are reading. Every contributing co-author has applied their knowledge and experiences. We have collectively experimented and produced *Finding your Moment Clarity*. Other examples are experimenting with going to college, take an online course, start building new positive relationships thru networking or explore entrepreneurship.

Entrepreneurship is the process of creating a product and or service that's available for sale in the marketplace and has the potential ability to solve a problem or issue. The telegraph, telephone, cell phone, computers, motorcar, space flight, stop light, straightening comb, automatic teller machines, and millions more all came from experiments.

Inventor Thomas Edison said: "I haven't failed; I've found 10,000 ways that won't work." Edison performed 10,000+ experiments in his lifetime before finding success.

Also, the flagship cleaning product that today is called Formula 409 was invented by Morris D. Rouff in 1957. History says that because of the persistence of two young Detroit scientist experimenting on 408 batches, their success came in the 409th batch or experiment. That is why the product was named Formula 409.

Experimenting is really just another way to say, take action! Success comes when you are persistent and don't give up.

THE FIVE HOUR RULE can transform how we think (failure or success), transform how we feel (we are good enough or not good enough), and most importantly, transform how we act (take action or watch television and allow life and opportunity to pass us by).

Listen to the sound of the opportunity clock: tick, tock, tick, tock, tick, tock. We all have the same twenty-four hours in a day. How we use our time (tick, tock, tick, tock) is what matters. Time waits for no one, so let's begin the habit of not wasting it!

If you are not where you want to be in life (I'm still reading and learning) give THE FIVE-HOUR RULE a chance to assist you on your quest to transform your life by reading, reflecting and experimenting. Pay special attention to the reflection that is staring back at you every time you look in the mirror. We are blessed and fortunate to be living in the information age that is right at our fingertips. We do not need to leave home (internet-google search) to research, all we need is a smartphone and an internet connection, and we are in business. We have come a long way from the one room school house.

Go to our website www.tmeginc.com to obtain our book titled Financially Speaking, and information on our online course.

In return, I have a free gift waiting for you-while they last. GO CLAIM YOUR FREE GIFT NOW AT www.tmeginc.com.

CHAPTER 24
FIVE-HOUR RULE EXERCISE

On your note pad or below, write down your list of the 5 activities that you will do EACH week to develop the Five-Hour Rule habit. Each number represents 1 hour of the week. Be specific. For example, I am going to read Financially Speaking for 1 hour on Mondays, I am going to meditate for 1 hour on Wednesdays.

1. _____

2. _____

3. _____

4. _____

5. _____

DEVELOP AN ABUNDANCE MINDSET

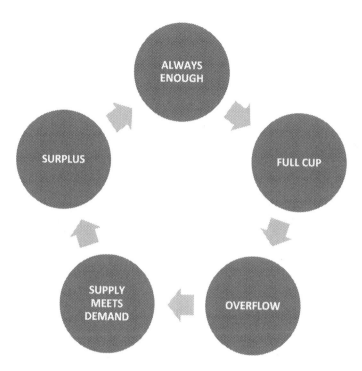

By Michael Bart Mathews

S econd to FEAR, Financially Speaking, money or the lack of money is the second biggest emotional baggage blocker that is a heavy weight on our shoulders. Not having enough money left over at the end of each month to pay the expenses, starts to create a variety of problems. Now a negative toll on the relationship capital begins to quietly seep into your daily thought process. Just as you have the ability to mentally rise above some of the unparalleled, falling negative aspects in other areas of your life, you must rise up and gain clarity around your finances! It is a critical part of "Finding Your Financial Moment of Clarity."

During the 2018 – 2019 USA government shutdown, it was heart-breaking to hear all of the stories from the employees and contractors that were living paycheck to paycheck. Thousands had to rely on food banks, family and friends to feed their families. Hundreds couldn't afford to put gas in their cars to even get to work as essential employees. Even though the shutdown lasted for only 35 days, some had to file for bankruptcy, as stated in several local and national news reports.

How many of you are living paycheck to paycheck? If you are, it's time for you to decide that you are going to be the captain of your personal finance ship, and the master of your financial thoughts. You must control what that little voice in your head when it tells you to spend and not save for the rainy days that seem to appear out of nowhere!

Some people have financial stinkin thinking because of the FEAR of failure. They are ashamed to let family, friends, co-workers, or business partners know that they are in financial trouble. So, they purchased things they don't need using OPM-other people's money, to impress people they don't like or know. In this case; MasterCard, Visa, and American Express credit cards become their lifeboat. These credit cards charge high interest rates (depending on your credit score) and an assortment of fees every time you are late with the payment. This is in addition to mortgage/rent payments, car payments, student loans, utilities, insurance, health care, child care, etc.

Also, some people due to their cultural upbringing have an aversion to money and wealth. They were taught that money is the root of all evil or money won't buy you happiness. Well, money is just a tool, and you can use it for good or evil, depending upon the type of person you want to be. And wouldn't you rather be happy with money than without, or at least wouldn't you like to find out for yourself? Don't let other people's opinion and limited beliefs about money become part of your mindset. Think for yourself.

And don't let the word "wealthy" scare you. Wealth means abundance. You define how much abundance you need and want in your life and get it!

Lastly, don't count on winning the lottery for lifelong financial stability. It is well known that a large percentage of people who win the lottery or get a big windfall actually end up broke in a few years. This is because they have no financial education or knowledge on how to preserve, grow and protect money. What makes you think you can handle millions if you can't manage $1,000 a month?

However, just as you need a plan to achieve your WHY, goal, purpose or dream, you need a plan to get your personal finances under control. If you continue to manage your money in the next five years, the same way you managed it in the past five years, how much money will you have? Here are some of the problems you may continue or begin to face:

➤ You will need to work 2 to 3 jobs to make ends meet
➤ You will continue to live paycheck to paycheck
➤ You spend all your savings trying to maintain your standard of living
➤ You dip into your retirement plan (if you have one) and if you are under age 59 and ½, you take a 10% early withdrawal penalty
➤ You rob Peter to pay Paul because the piper must be paid!
➤ You make high interest bearing cash advances on your credit cards, causing more debt to pile up on the current debt that you cannot pay
➤ You try to get a loan from the bank, family or friends, to no avail
➤ You get a loan at 400-800% from the payday loan company, and now you can't pay it back

➢ Stress and frustration from the lack of financial stability affects your health
➢ You begin to argue, fuss, and fight with your family due to lack of income, and mounting expenses
➢ In some situations, infidelity, alcohol and or drugs may enter the picture
➢ You file for bankruptcy trying to salvage the situation
➢ The car gets repossessed
➢ The house goes into foreclosure, and you eventually walk away
➢ Your personal credit score drops and negative entries are reported
➢ The divorce happens
➢ You become emotionally and financially bankrupt

There is hope. Financially Speaking, there is an abundance of personal financial literacy educational resources that can help eliminate many emotional, financial baggage blockers that affect you daily. Remember, your situation may be fixable. Like most situations, the way you think, act and feel either negative or positive will be your Financially Speaking guiding light towards financial success or self-destruction toward your financial failure!

There is no hocus pocus, abracadabra, get rich quick solutions to financial stability. It requires you to roll up your sleeves, make some sacrifices, put a plan together and stick to it. It will also help to have an accountability coach to keep you on task.

Personal finances are a subject that everyone seriously needs to know and understand. Nevertheless, people don't want to dig deep down to learn and understand how the financial game is played. You will need to educate yourself on key financial topics to be successful. Some key topics include:

1. Know Your Financial Numbers. Do You Know Your Net worth?

2. Know Your Health Numbers; Blood Pressure & Sugar, Cholesterol, PSA-Men.
3. Income from All Sources.
4. Saving/Investing: Emergency/Regular Savings Account/Mutual Funds.
5. Credit Management/Credit Score.
6. Debt/Expenses Management.
7. Wealth-Building and Preservation Strategies/Make Your Money Work for You.

Below are various resources to assist you in "Finding Your Moment of Financial Clarity" while in the comfort of your own time and space of your choosing. There need be no shame in learning the financial game!

My book titled "Financially Speaking: The Best Improvement Starts With Self Improvement-Create Your Own Economic Stimulus Plan is available on my website www.tmeginc.com or www.amazon.com.

My online course "Live W.E.A.L.T.H.Y.-7 Principles to Guide You on Your Journey to Abundance". Go to my website www. tmeginc.com for more information.

How to become financially independent by Earl Nightingale https://youtu.be/IrfQwcRkkzE. We live in the technology filled, information age. If you want that special something bad enough; take the next step.

Michael Bart Mathews interview on Financially Speaking: The Best Improvement Starts With Self Improvement-Create Your Own Economic Stimulus Plan https://youtu.be/ rwQ99S2C5Ac.

CHAPTER 25
DEVELOP AN ABUNDANCE MINDSET EXERCISE

On your note pad or below, write down your list of the 5 activities that you will do to improve your finances. For example, take the TMEG Live W.E.A.L.T.H.Y. online course, start a monthly/weekly savings plan with $$, cancel unnecessary subscriptions, find a better paying job, etc. The ways are endless. However, educating yourself and taking action is the key.

1. _____

2. _____

3. _____

4. _____

5. _____

CHAPTER 26

A NEW PARADIGM LED BY PHENOMENAL WOMEN

By Michael Bart Mathews

To my wife Robbie, and to all the amazing, very remarkable, extraordinary, empowering phenomenal women around the world who are change agents. I want to give you praise for being that special someone who is loving, caring, sharing, supporting, and most importantly, highly qualified. Keep showcasing your many gifts and talents for the greater good of humanity in our global community.

Throughout history; from the Suffragette's to the #Me Too Movement and The Global Women Clubs, women all around the world are making the shift to new paradigms in large numbers. Women are no longer staying under the preverbal glass ceiling or staying confined in the imaginary box while sitting on the sidelines in the game of life.

For years, women are choosing no longer to stay at home. A vast amount of thought leadership guided Phenomenal Women, actively participate in the game of life with one mission; to win in spite of or along with, and even without men. Whether she be a single woman or a married woman, she is thriving because she made the decision and choose to shift her thinking to a new paradigm of thought. The Phenomenal Woman is displaying thought leadership while competing in the male-dominated corporate boardrooms, small business ownership, and political arenas across the globe.

She is climbing the unequal ladder while building-growing-and sustaining wealth by starting her own ultra-successful business. She is creating products and services that are available in the global marketplace.

For my female thought leaders; take a stroll through your mind by thinking back to your own personal a-ha or breakthrough moments along your journey. Think about the opposition that you faced in the board room. Think about the discouragement, the unequal treatment and sometimes not being listened to at all.

Imagine and think about all the women who started to believe they could compete on a higher level and become successful because you blazed the trail that they now can follow. Think about had you not walked that journey until you succeed, how many other women who watched you, and because of your success, they made the paradigm shift and got in the race for equality, opportunity and their own success?

RUTH BADER GINSBURG; Associate Justice of the Supreme Court of the United States – "How fortunate I was to be alive and a lawyer when, for the first time in the United States history, it became possible to urge, successfully, before legislators and courts, the equal-citizenship stature of women and men as a fundamental constitutional principle."

For those of you who have yet to do so, think about the endless struggles along your journey. What if you bowed down to conformity, and did not throw your crown into the ring of leadership? Where, in life, would you be today?

Think about and do your own due diligence, and research the accomplishments of the following women, who represent yet a small fraction of the tip of the iceberg of the many women who are on a mission to win in spite of men. I'll only name the top 10 wealthiest women in the United States as of the writing of this publication. And as you can see, they all have reached the billionaire plateau on the financial level.

If becoming a billionaire is not one of your shooting stars for financial success; that's fine. If becoming a millionaire is not one of your shooting starts for success, that's fine also. However, at least shoot for financial abundance.

My point for listing billionaire women is to showcase the simple fact that women can, have, and are becoming billionaires, just like men. True, men dominate the overall list. However, women are shifting their financial paradigm within the global economy and more and more are leveling up and becoming members of the millionaire and billionaire's clubs.

Some were born with that proverbial silver spoon (generational wealth-old money) in their mouths, while others came from less fortunate circumstances such as poverty or being immigrants here in America. This list came from a Forbes report; however, it is not a full representation of the female billionaires that exist worldwide:

- Alice Walton - Walmart
- Jacqueline Mars - Mars Candy Company
- Laurence Powell Jobs - Owns Apple Shares
- Abigail Pierrepont Johnson - CEO of Fidelity Investments
- Blair Parry-Okeden - Owns Shares in Cox Enterprises
- Marion Ilitch - Founder of Little Caesars Pizza & Ilitch Holdings
- Diane Hendricks - ABC Supply Roofing Company
- Oprah Winfrey - O Magazine/OWN Network
- Jin Sook Chang - Founder of Forever 21 Clothing Store
- Christy Walton - Wal-Mart shares & First Solar investments
- Diane Kemper - Real Estate investor

There is a survey that says that 36% of female billionaires in the United States are younger than 40, and they take great pride in themselves for having self-made fortunes.

To all the powerful and empowering Phenomenal Women from around the world who are reading this book, I salute you, and I tip my hat to you! Think about and imagine yourself now being on the Forbes list of billionaires. However, with these words, I'm strictly talking to the empowering Phenomenal Women with thought leadership and vision to walk the walk of winning just like men, in spite of all the many obstacles that present a challenge of failure vs. success.

Think about and imagine how many men that support (some men always have opposed) your thought leadership and contributions in the industry of your choice, for the betterment of our global community. I am just one of many who publicly and openly supports each and every one of you along your journey.

I am a feminist in thought. I believe that men and women should be treated equally in the game of life. I've met many empowering women from around the world who display a high level of thought leadership, while she walks her

Phenomenal Woman journey throughout life. Some are single (with or without children), some are in a relationship, others are married and have children to raise. Regardless of her situation, countless women leaders are becoming more and more Phenomenal!

I am in no way putting my male readers down in this chapter, however, I am most defiantly shinning the bright, illuminating light of empowerment on all women who seize this moment in time and continue to step out of the shadows and shine their bright guided thought leadership light in our global community around the world.

Food for thought: think about the empowering women thought leaders that you personally know that has influenced your desire and enhanced your belief about you being able to be, do, and have that specific special something that you seek.

I've met a fair number of empowering women from many different countries. I have shared the stage with some, written books and magazine articles with others, invested with some, and currently working on projects with others. The beauty of their empowerment and capabilities are never-ending.

MY TRIBUTE TO THE PHENOMENAL GLOBAL WOMAN

I believe that many great male leaders, who have been inspired by an empowering Phenomenal Woman, has experienced an enormous amount of success.

When things in life get tough, as they sometimes will, you may be deserted by family and those who you thought were friends. The Phenomenal Woman will always be in the trenches with you through thick and thin when need be!

When you have a Phenomenal Woman by your side, you'll never be alone. She'll be willing to start over again if necessary, with or without you! She will share her vision with a new enthusiasm that comes from her thought leadership and faith in you, as well as the empowering faith that she has in herself. The Phenomenal Woman will not remain idle. She will not sit on the sidelines, nor will she take a back seat and watch you fail! Nor will she accept failure for herself! If necessary, she will lead or walk by your side in partnership.

Having someone to love and having someone to share your success and accomplishments with is vital.

The Phenomenal Woman will provide praise (pat on the back) or constructive criticism (kick in the butt) when needed from time to time. A man can become successful without a wife, life partner & family. However, all the real joy is taken out of it. Take care of yourself Phenomenal Woman, because it's quite obvious that the world really needs you!

> *"It's beautiful when you find your path to your own destiny – A new paradigm for changing the world."*
> *-Mirela Sula*

GLOBAL WOMAN LEADERS ROCK

She is a global woman with a new paradigm for changing the world
She helps business women, young ladies, and growing little girls
She is an empowering global woman leader, operating outside of the box
She is business savvy and extremely smart like a fox
She leads with foresight because hindsight won`t do
She moves her agenda forward, and her vision is true
She is a quick-witted, leader with blood vessels of steel
She makes hard decisions, sometimes wearing high heels
She leads with her left, other times with her right
She`s doubted in the board room, backing down from no fight
She`s in the 15th round and still standing strong
She has leadership skills so she can`t go wrong
She knows the secret that makes her a global woman leader
She fully understands that the world really needs her
She has patience and understanding, she will leave you in the dust
She is a symbol of beauty and brains, and worthy of worlds trust
She doesn`t stand around waiting for opportunity to knock
Because she is an empowering **GLOBAL WOMAN LEADER,** who definitely **Rocks!**

-**Michael Bart Mathews**

CHAPTER 27

EPILOGUE

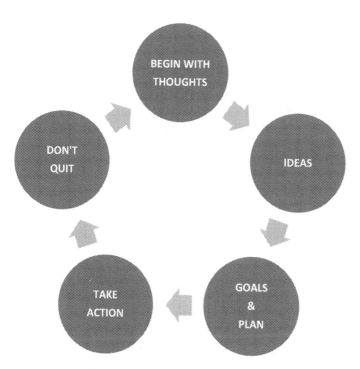

By Michael Bart Mathews

"I only hope that we don't lose sight of one thing –
that it was all started by a mouse."
-Walt Disney

T he most important next step along your journey is to never give up and don't you quit!

Imagine and seriously think about having your own world-changing Mickey Mouse-like idea.

Imagine from your thoughts you identified and singled out your own vision for success. Think about how you first visualized the finished product before you got started toward completion.

Imagine right now today, at this very moment, you are reviewing your written plan of action for achievement. Imagine you have created your outline, or prototype because you took your thought from your mind and went to the drawing board-the written beginning of your creative thought.

> *"First comes thought; then organization of thought into ideas and plans; then transforming those plans into reality. The beginning, as you will observe, is in your Imagination."*
> -Napoleon Hill

Now imagine going through any and all obstacles and not quitting in spite of the non-believers, nay-sayers, and haters, who are all watching from the sidelines.

Imagine from your creation from thought, you turned your new idea into a visible, tangible, product or service.

Imagine and think about your thoughts being organized for accomplishment from the structured plans that you now have. Imagine your written down plans have become your everyday new reality. Imagine you are actually living your ideas, goals, and dreams today, in the present time.

Seriously think about this for a moment before you read on!

NOW THAT YOU HAVE A CLEAR VISION

Imagine your newly created "that special something" is available on an e-commerce website or throughout the distribution channels of other worldwide companies. Imagine you are sitting in your living room, and you receive an alert indicating someone on a different continent has purchased your product or service. Imagine person after person after person doing the same thing over and over again.

Think about and imagine, because you achieved "that special something" others around you now share in your achievement because you took the first step and persisted until you succeed. You did not quit. Imagine you are now able to offer family, friends, and others a hand up instead of a handout. Imagine changing the lives of our global community because you succeeded.

Think about what would happen to all those people who you just helped, had you not achieved "that special something." Imagine and think about all the people you will be letting down if you quit and don't succeed.

It's time to shed your old skin of indecision and take your new first step toward transformation and personal achievement that is your birthright. Looking introspectively into your thought process will be very challenging. However, this introspective mirror image of self-reflection can also be very rewarding. Dive deep down within your mental capacity, and mind-map from thought, until you first visualize, and next create, your own world changing, Walt Disney-Mickey Mouse type of idea. Napoleon Hill: "Everything begins with an idea." First we must think "IT," in order to create and achieve "IT."

Become a winner and don't let anyone steal your dreams. Most importantly, don't allow your self – reflection, the one staring back at you every time you look in the mirror, become the person who actually steals your dream.

Imagine you developed the necessary skills required to tap into your internal guidance system. Imagine your intuition is now guiding you in the direction of your internal thoughts while transforming those thoughts into your physical, tangible realities.

Imagine you are still the same humble, grateful, person who now has an abundance of financial success because you have achieved "that special something," Imagine being in a self-imposed servant leadership position because you can now afford to serve others at a higher level.

Seriously think about and imagine taking your first step on your one-thousand mindset mile shifting journey. Now imagine completing the final step of your journey, and you have finally arrived at that place in life that first began in your thoughts. Would you agree that from the outset, your idea seemed like it was a far-far-far-far away place in your mind? But with each thought, and with each step, one thought at a time and one step at a time, you are now exactly where you thought about being in life. You have become exactly who you thought about becoming in life.

YOUR THOUGHTS AND ACTIONS DETERMINE YOUR SUCCESS OR FAILURE:

> ➤ *"Whether you think you can, or think you can't – you're right" – Henry Ford*
> ➤ *"I don't believe in circumstances. The people who get along in this world are the people who get up and look for the circumstances they want, and if they can't find them, they make them" - George Bernard Shaw*
> ➤ *"I will persist until I succeed. I was not delivered into this world in defeat, nor does failure course in my veins. I am not a sheep waiting to be prodded by my shepherd. I am a lion, and I refuse to talk, to walk, to sleep with the sheep. The slaughterhouse of failure is not my destiny. I will persist until I succeed." -Og Mandino*

There is no magic bullet, no fairytale happy ending without doing the work.

> *"Positive thought without positive action is only wishful thinking. Positive results from positive thought are only possible with correlated positive actions. "*
> *— Robbie Mathews*

YOUR CALL TO ACTION
NOW THAT YOU FOUND YOUR
"MOMENT OF CLARITY," GO OUT THERE
AND CHANGE THE WORLD!

ABOUT THE CO-AUTHORS

NATALIE M. BONOMO (UNITED STATES)

Photo by Sara Durham
Motivational Speaker, Author

N ATALIE M. BONOMO is dedicated to leading and inspiring others to shift their paradigms so they may realize their potential and ability to achieve and exceed their dreams of health, wealth, happiness, and service to others. A lifelong learner and student of Wayne Dyer, Abraham Hicks, Napoleon Hill, Stephen Covey, and Tony Robbins to name a few, Natalie is an organizational development professional, a humanitarian, and a motivational speaker and author on self-actualization and living inspired.

Natalie is no stranger to positive thinking and focusing on living in the vortex. "Throughout my life, whenever I was faced with adversity, my internal guidance would redirect me to finding the positive in any situation, appreciating it for what it taught me, and moving forward. Often criticized by others for my genuine desire to focus on the good, I learned to embrace my differences and dance to the rhythm of my own music."

Her introduction to teaching and energy work started in the late eighties when she became a student of the Korean martial art of Hapkido. In 1990, she earned a 1st Degree Black Belt and served as a martial arts instructor for nearly a decade. Dedicated to excellence, she was no stranger to the "dojo," often practicing seven days a week and competing in tournaments.

In 1992, Natalie earned a bachelor's degree in Organizational/ Corporate Communications with a minor in Spanish from Northern Illinois University. Going to work for a Fortune 500 pharmaceutical company, she was introduced to Stephen Covey's 7 Habits of Highly Effective People and fell in love with Covey's approach to achieving excellence and living a balanced life. It was during that time that Natalie felt a calling to help others achieve their greatest potential and she embarked on her journey in making this dream a reality as she became certified to teach Covey's 7 Habits.

Over the next two decades, her career evolved in the field of corporate training and organizational development. Moving from pharmaceuticals to servant leadership in municipal government, her true passion for coaching and inspiring others to be their best and watching them grow really flourished.

Desiring a deeper connection with her higher consciousness, Natalie became Reiki certified in 2016. Later that year, she initiated her formal writing experience where she first wrote about the vortex and mindfulness as a co-author in *Finding Your Moment of Clarity: Discovering Your Power Within*. Toward the end of 2016, Natalie joined Toastmasters International and discovered yet another passion, motivational speaking. Toastmasters allowed her the opportunity to become a coach on public speaking design and delivery. She was also gifted the opportunity to share material from her new thought-provoking and inspiring guidebook, *Your Greatest Potential! Master Your Thinking, Create the Life You Desire*, and witness the emotional impact and lasting effects it played upon her audience as they attentively listened to, grew from, and enthusiastically cheered on each new speech.

"Inspired by what had awakened within my soul, I felt a burning desire to continue writing and was granted the privilege, yet again, to work with Michael Bart Mathews. Thank you, 'Big Mike,' for your contribution to Chapter 4 titled, "We Become What We Think About" in my book. Anticipated to be available mid-2019 via Barnes & Noble, Amazon, and major online retailers worldwide, *Your Greatest Potential!* takes you through an introspective journey to master your thinking and open yourself to opportunity.

This inspiring guidebook is about discovering and feeding the fire of passion that burns within you, so you may live with purpose and be the best possible version of you. *Your Greatest Potential!* enables you to: 1) conduct an "autopsy" of your thinking to reveal and remove obstacles affecting how you think, feel, and act which are causing you to struggle or lack the passion and purpose you desire; 2) shift your mindset and behavior to align with your values; and 3) address anything that may be interfering with your ability to unleash your hidden treasures, achieve *your* greatest potential, and exceed your dreams. *Your Greatest Potential!* outlines practices to open your mind to an effective way of thinking and assist you in breaking paradigms that are misaligned from your innate desires allowing you to replace them with ones that serve your greatest purpose, therefore, enabling you to take charge of your life and increase your ability to attract what you truly desire.

Connect with Natalie Bonomo via LinkedIn to build your "like-minded, positive thinking, high achievers" database; for details on *Your Greatest Potential!* publication; or to work with Natalie as a coach for Accountability (personal/professional goal setting/achievement), Public Speaking (design/delivery) or Writing (book/resume/website content/technical).

May you forever tap into the universe of dreams to achieve *your* greatest potential, and may you contribute to the ripple effect by sharing your gifts and talents with the world.

Blessings, Natalie

Natalie Bonomo/Accountability Coach
Public Speaker-Writer
Author of *Your Greatest Potential:*
Master Your Thinking-Create the Life You Desire
United States
natalie.bonomo@yahoo.com

Peter Diaz (Australia)

Photo by Elle Stojanovska
Founder-CEO-Workplace Mental Health Institute
Accredited Mental Health Social Worker

P eter Diaz is founder and CEO and of the Workplace Mental Health Institute (WMHI). An Accredited Mental Health Social Worker by profession, Peter is a highly respected international speaker on the topic of workplace mental health, resilience, the role of leadership in creating psychologically safe workplaces and emotional intelligence. He is also the author of *Mental Wealth – A Managers Guide to Workplace Mental Health and Wellbeing* and *Reclaim Your Power*.

Peter's professional experience includes positions as a psychological injury expert for GIO Insurance, a visiting fellow at the University of Wollongong, a field educator for the Australian Catholic University, and the NSW President of the Australian Association of Social Workers. He has worked in community mental health services as a senior manager, where he is known for his expertise in change management and the development of recovery-oriented programs and workforces.

He's also seen the damage that unattended mental health issues can have not only for the person experiencing them, but also for those around them, including colleagues, family, and friends.

Peter's mission is to revolutionize the way mental health is approached around the world, by providing cutting edge, unique and honest education programs to workplaces that get real results—both for the business and the people in it.

Peter has helped Fortune 500 companies increase profits by enhancing the mental health, wellbeing, resilience and productivity of their workforce. He's helped thousands of people and businesses become empowered so they can thrive.

He has interviewed business giants like Steve Wozniak (co-founder of Apple), and Randi Zuckerberg (marketing genius behind Facebook) on the topics of employee engagement, workplace wellbeing, and resilience. And he has featured in numerous media publications including BBC, SBS, ABC, *Business Insider, Daily Telegraph* and *Woman's Day*.

Website: https://www.thepeterdiaz.com/
Contact Peter at peter@thepeterdiaz.com
LinkedIn: https://www.linkedin.com/in/thepeterdiaz/

ADAKU EZEUDO (IRELAND)

Photo by Guy James
Founder-Director-PhoenixRize
Author, Diversity and Inclusion Consultant,
Trainer, Coach, Mentor

Adaku Ezeudo is a Diversity and Inclusion Consultant, Trainer, Mentor and Coach and has worked across functions in multinationals and public sector organizations before starting a transformation boutique consultancy called PhoenixRize Consulting where she specializes in supporting organizations in meeting their statutory Equality and Diversity requirements.

She also founded i-Smile International, a charity set up in Ireland and Nigeria to enhance the economic, political, cultural and social participation of marginalized women. She has received multiple awards and recognition for her work on social inclusion, community activation, women empowerment both locally and Internationally. In 2018, she was listed as one of Dublin's Heroes and one of the most exceptional and inspiring people in Dublin by the Dublin City Council Culture Company.

Adaku is on a mission to help purpose driven women to create a life they love so they can make an impact, fulfill their purpose and turn passion to profit. She is a listener, a doer and a woman driven by compassion, faith, a fierce sense of justice and a heart full of love. Adaku believes that dreamers change the world and it is possible to live your dream, this inspired her to co-author an internationally recognized bestselling book 'Mission Critical Messengers', where she contributed a chapter titled – 'How to Live Your Dream Year' in collaboration with 11 world-class authors.

Often referred to as the lady with the infectious smile, Adaku finds humor in everyday situations. One of her favorite quotes is "life is not a dress rehearsal, so don't waste your precious time doing things that don't light your fire." Adaku is an encourager, an unshakeable optimist and a transformational speaker. She uses her personal stories to inspire others to take action and rise to their fullest potential.

She sits on the board of management for a number of charity organizations and is part of several consultative forums in Ireland. She holds a master's degree in Development Studies from Kimmage Development Studies Centre, Dublin, a Post Graduate Certificate in Women, Gender and Social Justice from University College Dublin and a Post Graduate Certificate in Race & Ethnicity from Trinity College Dublin.

She is a mother of 3 gorgeous girls.

Adaku Ezeudo - Founder/Director
PhoenixRize Consulting/Diversity & Inclusion Consulting
| Dublin 15 | 0879641229 | Ireland
info@phoenixrize.ie

Elyse Falzone (United States)

Photo by Megan Sherer
Intuitive Healer and Spiritual Life Coach

Elyse Falzone is an Intuitive Healer and Spiritual Life Coach who empowers women to be leaders in their families, communities and beyond. Elyse believes we are each teachers, healers, and lightworkers in our own unique way. Through her own struggles, Elyse embarked on a journey of self-discovery, self-expression, and awakening to her soul's Divine gifts. She now pays this forward and holds sacred space for her clients to awaken to their spiritual gifts and talents so they can share them with the world.

Through a spiritual and intuitive framework, and techniques such as Energy Healing, Meditation, Emotional Intelligence, Yoga, Reiki, Angel Readings, Crystals, Sound Healing and more, Elyse connects with her clients through an immersive & interactive experience. She guides them to let go, forgive and heal so they can take a journey to honor their inner voice and live out their life's calling and souls' purpose each and every day.

Elyse also serves as a Spiritual Guide and Mentor for business professionals, CEOs and business owners who are striving to lead from a connected, heart-centered place and are seeking alignment for self and business.

Elyse is the creator and facilitator of the Certified Healers Course and is sought out as a master energy healer and guest expert for retreats, workshops, and stages around the world.

Elyse Falzone
Intuitive Healer & Spiritual Life Coach
www.elysefalzone.com
IG: @_awakenyoursoul
FB: @awakenyoursoulglobal

EMI GOLDING (AUSTRALIA)

Photo by Elle Stojanovska
Founder-Workplace Mental Health
Institute, Psychologist, Consultant

E mi Golding is the Celebrity Psychologist, Fortune 500 Consultant on the creation of mentally wealthy workplaces and Founder of the Workplace Mental Health Institute. A member of the Australian Psychological Society, Emi has many years' experience in the mental health sector, working on the frontline and in senior management positions, as well as with individuals in private practice.

Emi has an extensive understanding of the complexities of mental disorders and what is needed to overcome them, as well as how to prevent mental ill health by building personal resilience and strategies for high performance and wellbeing.

Emi was an expert panel member for the development of guidelines for organizations on the prevention of mental disorders in the workplace, and she is particularly passionate about suicide prevention. She regularly provides consultation to organizations on the psychological safety of their workplaces.

An accomplished businesswoman, Emi has been recognized as Top Female Entrepreneur 2018, by global magazine Woman Entrepreneur, and Emi has spoken on stages in the USA, Australia, Europe, and South Africa. She regularly collaborates with high-level business partners around the world and has met with and interviewed celebrities including Dr. Phil, Randi Zuckerberg, Bethenny Frankel and many more.

Emi is an author, international speaker and has been featured in global publications including CLEO magazine, *HealthTimes*, and the book, *Fear to Freedom*.

Website: https://www.emigolding.com/
Contact Emi at emi@emigolding.com
LinkedIn: https://www.linkedin.com/in/emigolding/

About Workplace Mental Health Institute

The Workplace Mental Health Institute is a global organisation, specialising in helping organisations to improve their productivity and profitability by ensuring the psychological safety of their workplaces.

The Workplace Mental Health Institute offers complete workplace wellbeing solutions for improving employee engagement, productivity, and business results.

The Workplace Mental Health Institute partners with corporate, governments, and community organisations across the world, to assess their psychological risk profiles, identify the root cause of any problems, develop an evidence-based plan of action, and implement it effectively to get tangible results for the people and the bottom line.

Its mission is to strengthen people and organisations from the inside out, by delivering strength-based mental health education and consultation that is refreshingly honest, unique and gets results fast.

Website: https://www.wmhi.com.au/
Email: admin@wmhi.com.au

Marja Katajisto (Switzerland)

Photo by Denise Ackerman
Freelance Writer and Photographer

Marja Katajisto is a present day happy Mother, a freelance writer, and a photographer.

She is passionate about capturing joy and happiness, natural beauty and the love of life in its many forms.

Before moving to Switzerland with her husband and two daughters, she had another long career in business and marketing in her native country, Finland.

Ending her career there as the Chief of Marketing (COM) in a 60-plus strong Shopping Center gave her a role and a voice as a local, public figure in Vaasa.

Marja was a Board Member in several associations, and offices focused on developing and improving the business, logistics, and attractiveness of the commercial city center. During this time, she created communal programs and campaigns (E.g., Rewell Storm, CityKids, Vorovek) to address the commerce or disciplinary and public challenges in the heart of the city.

Marja believes that the only medicine for all eyesores of the humankind is the loving and supporting parenting leading to mutual respect and appreciation.

"How frustrating it is to see, that great efforts and resources worldwide are dedicated to finding ways to cope with the results of inadequate upbringing, instead of fixing the causes. Also, it is unfortunate when educational curriculums are not guaranteed to discover and accommodate the interests and life-carrying talents of <u>every</u> child. It's frustrating when we as responsible adults can discover, yet choose to become blind towards crippling "neglect." Indeed, the cure always needs to be lovingly poured on the young roots and the soil around them."

The saying goes: "In our children, we see our future." But Marja wonders if we really understand what all that entails? It is we who choose the colors for that future. It is we who need to be present for our children NOW. We adults should be good role models and should show support, endless love, and genuine inspiration and thus, very likely, bring out the best in children and in people around us. How guided education can be transformational (rather than weakness-seeking) actually truly can motivate and propel children into a roaring hunger of wanting to learn more, and more! And thus, no-one becomes a drop-out!

Marja wants us to create lasting positive changes in humanity, with loads of positive ripple-effects! – "I really can't see any other way working," she says and smiles kindly, as her eyes are filled with comforting hope.

"Gratitude and Kindness are the highest forms of human intelligence. I wish that insightful and mature decision making on all levels would bring unwavering results. I wish integrity, encouraging accountability, and a strong sense of responsibility for results and genuine care." In short, Marja thinks that it is high time to restore humanity with a more caring concept,

216

always constructive, free from judging and destruction. In our hearts we all know, she says, that the cure starts on an individual level. – "And it will spread out like the mighty force of a wildfire, once we truly absorb and embrace the great <u>motivation</u> and reward hidden talents in everyone therein."

In Switzerland, during her 10 years as a multitasking homemaker, Marja learned to fully tap into the ultimate wisdom of living out one's talents and potentials, in order to be able to contribute to the shared balance and well-being of her family. Not having to be a breadwinner; being free from the rat race where she too once was; really opened her eyes. Experiencing that kind of freedom brought clarity to her life philosophy and polished her unwavering belief in everyone's sublime uniqueness and therefore, deriving mission. - "To me, parenthood is and has been the very best educator. It molds and hones a person. It replaces selfishness with elastic leniency. It teaches how love is omnipotent and how it, in fact, is THE way that will guide people to their purpose and highest mission, eventually leading them to happiness and fulfillment."

For Marja, to bring up the next generation and to even be able to set the temperature for the one coming after them, is the greatest honor. – "I don't think that there is any other task more important than this one in our world."

Marja Katajisto is a big fan of the amazing concept of Life, she loves and respects our unique Nature and has developed a lasting fondness for seaside living. – "I always wish to live by water - the saltier, the better."

She is a keen dancer, enjoys interior designing and likes fitness.

Her family and friends know her as a natural-born optimizer, and as someone who brainstorms and solves problems of all scopes.

217

She is also the co-founder and Board Member in Geneswiss Consultancy GmbH, (Zürich), which offers "Leadership 2 Success" Coaching worldwide in English, Swedish and Finnish.

Marja Katajisto is currently working on a project that combines her photography, her literal production, and her life-philosophies. - Thank you for reading!

Marja Katajisto:
Co-Founder of Geneswiss Consultancy
Photographer & Writer
www.marjak.me
Marja@marjak.me
Marja.Katajisto@geneswiss.com

Robbie Mathews (United States)

Photo by Jerome Lynch
President-The Mathew Entrepreneur Group, Inc
Financial Wellness Transformation Coach,
International Speaker, Author

As seen on ANN7 BizPulse Television (South Africa); 93.8FM Radio (South Africa); Kaya FM95.5 Radio (South Africa); Saturday Star & Sunday Times (South Africa); Global Women Magazines (London); London Business Magazine (London), The Business Woman Today Magazine (London), Radio France (France); LVH-Las Vegas Hollywood Magazine (United States); The Dubaian Magazine (Dubai); 102.3FM Radio (United States) CANN TV (United States), Global Woman TV (London).

Robbie S. Mathews is a successful global entrepreneur, an empowering international speaker, financial education and transformation coach, author and an investor. She is the editor and contributing writer for their 2016 self-published book, the second edition of, *Financially Speaking: The Best Improvement Starts with Self-Improvement-Create Your Own Economic Stimulus Plan*. Which became the cornerstone that formed her company's financial education wings.

Robbie is co-founder and President of The Mathews Entrepreneur Group, Inc (TMEG). The company is headquartered in Chicago, Illinois in the United States. It was founded in 2007 by Robbie and her husband, Michael Bart Mathews-CEO. They specialize in personal financial literacy education, coaching, accountability and empowerment strategies using books, workshops, seminars, one-on-one coaching, and online programs.

She has spoken about the importance of financial literacy education publicly in the United States and internationally. "Financial literacy education is not a priority in our school systems. So, it is important that the issue is addressed by all of us and at all levels of society."

Robbie and Michael provide their clients with the knowledge and strategies to help them manage their personal and small business finances, so they can get out and stay out of debt, spend guilt-free and live financially free.

Robbie spoke in front of a crowd of over 1,200+ attendees from 20+ countries in Johannesburg, South Africa. During her speech, she shared their global message about the need for personal financial literacy education. In addition, Robbie interviewed Nelson Mandela's grandson, Ndaba Mandela on stage regarding how the South African people can change their economic culture.

Robbie is a co-author of a book and a participant in an upcoming PBS Television special both titled: *Phenomenal Global Women.* She along with 10 other women from different countries, cultures, and nationalities share their life stories, their journeys, and their experiences. Their mission is to inspire, motivate and empower all women around the world.

Robbie has 40 years of Information Technology development and management experience within the retail and financial services industry. She earned her bachelor's degree in

Business and master's degree in Information Systems. During these years, she served as a diversity and inclusion advocate and global mentor. Robbie traveled to London and Dublin Ireland on several business trips while being employed at the Vice President level. She retired from a Chicago based Fortune 500 international financial services firm in 2014.

Robbie is committed to giving back both time and money to the community. She has donated for years to the Historically Black Colleges and Universities, the United Way and other charitable organizations. Her investment group has donated over 3 million sandwiches to the community.

In addition to winning numerous awards for Quality and Diversity Advocacy during her tenure in financial services, Robbie won the Inspirational Global Woman Award in London in 2017.

She has been featured on live television, magazines, podcast, and newspapers internationally and locally. Robbie also graces the cover of Global Woman Magazine based in London.

Robbie and Michael are available to conduct workshops, seminars, speaking engagements and personalized coaching for individuals, small business and corporate wellness programs.

Robbie and Michael reside in Illinois and enjoy writing, traveling and spending time with their grandchildren.

Website: www.tmeginc.com
Facebook: https://www.facebook.com/robbiesmathews
Facebook: https://www.facebook.com/tmegroupinc
LinkedIn: https://www.linkedin.com/in/robbiesmathews/

AMY SAYAMA (UNITED STATES)

Photo by Amy Sayama
Certified Deepak Chopra Perfect Health Instructor

Amy Sayama is a Certified Laughter Yoga Teacher, author, homeschool educator, and NLP modalities educator.

For more than forty years, Amy has developed her deep passion for teaching. Young students learned sensory experiences from developmental early childhood education. K-12 students are taught the NLP style of learning for the homeschool interest driven subjects. Amy is certified in integrated health for people of all ages. She focuses on balancing the 24-hour day through eating nutritious foods, getting the proper sleep, diminishing the work overload and adding play and laughter.

As the saying goes, Laughter is the best medicine. Amy is also a certified Laughter Yoga teacher which enables her to lead classes in playful exercises, and she is also able to certify others to lead classes for people of all ages as well.

Amy is the author of her book titled: *Bravest Journey*. It's a book of quotes. Her book takes a plunge into life's journey, the bravest journey. Inside most of our fears of being scared of life's unknowns, that holds us back is the bravest journey wanting to burst out triumphantly. Amy's book has Ninety-nine eloquent quotes to help you embark on your bravest journey in the life that you seek. Her book encourages us to step out of the dark shadows, and into the bright illuminating light of transformation. Being brave changes an ordinary day into an extraordinary experience.

Amy Sayama
Certified Laughter Yoga Teacher
Certified Deepak Chopra Center Instructor
Author of *Bravest Journey*
Email: amysayama@gmail.com
Website: www.amysayama.com

KAREL VERMEULEN (SOUTH AFRICA)

Photo by Destiny Man Magazine/Freelance Photographer
Entrepreneur, International Speaker, Wealth Coach, Author

Karel Vermeulen is a serial entrepreneur, international inspirational speaker, wealth coach, and published author. He is also known as coach karelv or the entrepreneur guru. His vision and mission are, to inspire and motivate people to take immediate action and full responsibility for their own success and destiny. He is the owner and developer of the globally successful brand Lubrimaxxx personal lubricant and managing director of Erabella Hair Extensions. He also is a co-owner of Continuum Coffee Shop, co-owner of Hamilton Garden Suites, where they rent out high quality affordable short stay accommodation for business travelers and one of two shareholders at Communimail (www. communimail.com), a semi-automated customer engagement and relationship building tool in the form of a newsletter that is informative, engaging and makes your clients feel special while you focus on growing your business.

He has been featured in various magazines, interviewed on radio stations and has a weekly radio slot called Your Monday BizWiz on radio channel 94.fm in South Africa. This show focuses on everything regarding business and entrepreneur principles. He holds regular small accountability group sessions at his house, where he teaches other entrepreneurs and small business owners the value and importance of accountability, entrepreneur principles, and mindset coaching. His YouTube channel launched in February 2019 called TheKVZone is a platform where he interviews regular ordinary people that share their success stories to inspire and motivate others. It is also a teaching platform where he imparts business and entrepreneur knowledge to help people to achieve success in all aspects of their lives. He knows the importance of having a business coach because he currently retains six coaches who guide and hold him accountable in reaching his objectives and goals.

He is the first South African author to be published by New York publishers Morgan James with his book title *Do You Really Want To Be An Entrepreneur?* The subtitle of his book is "How I created a seven-figure business in twenty-four months from my kitchen table." This book is available from Amazon, various bookstores and airport outlets in North America, Canada, United Kingdom, and South Africa as well as 1800 other online platforms. His eBook *How To Expand Your Brand* is available as a free download from his website www. thekvbrand.com.

He was not always an entrepreneur. Throughout his career path, he held many positions, from a police sergeant, a missionary, and working in the mining industry, to serving high-profile ministers and ambassadors as head butler for the Ritz-Carlton Hotel in Bahrain. These are just a few of the many occupations he's had. Living a healthy lifestyle is important, and he loves nature and appreciates good music and fine wine. He currently lives happily with his life partner in Cape Town, South Africa. He has a serving heart, and his greatest pleasure in life is to see other people succeed.

Through trial and error, he learned the secrets of becoming a millionaire. He made his first million at the age of forty-two, and he believes that it's never too late for anyone to make their first million. His motto is "Your Results, Our Success," which speaks volumes of his true character.

Follow Karel Vermeulen here:
Facebook: https://www.facebook.com/karel.vermeulen
LinkedIn: https://www.linkedin.com/in/
karel-vermeulen-30a06a87/
Twitter: https://www.twitter.com/coachKarelV
Instagram: https://www.instagram.com/vermeulen.karel/
TheKVZone YouTube Channel:
https://studio.youtube.com/channel/
UCl7wgUB7fUFw76_VEZ6yk7w

Websites:
https://www.thekvbrand.com
https://www.15hamilton.co.za
https://www.lubrimaxxx.com
https://www.erabellahair.com

Purchase his book through Amazon link:
https://www.amazon.com/You-Really-Want-Entrepreneur-Seven-figure/dp/1642792187/ref=tmm_pap_swatch_0?_enco
ding=UTF8&qid=1547915717&sr=8-1

Personal Email: karel@thekvbrand.com

ABOUT THE LEAD AUTHOR

MICHAEL BART MATHEWS
(UNITED STATES)

Photo by The Mathews Entrepreneur Group
CEO-The Mathews Entrepreneur Group
Financial Wellness Transformation Coach,
International Speaker, Author

As seen on ANN7 BizPulse Television (South Africa); 93.8FM Radio (South Africa); Kaya FM95.5 Radio (South Africa); Saturday Star & Sunday Times News Papers (South Africa); Global Women-Global Man Magazines (London); WORKLIFE Magazine (Australia); LVH-Las Vegas Hollywood Magazine (United States); The Dubian Magazine (Dubai); 102.3FM Radio (United States) CANN TV (United States); Business Booster Today (Germany) and Radio France (France).

Michael "Bart" Mathews is a successful global Entrepreneur, Investor, Published Author, Personal Growth & Development Financial Education Coach, Celebrity Interviewer, and International Speaker.

Michael and his wife Robbie are co-founders of The Mathews Entrepreneur Group (TMEG). They are dedicated and committed to providing Personal Development & Financial Literacy educational programs using his book titled; Financially Speaking: The Best Improvement Starts With Self-Improvement-Create Your Own Economic Stimulus Plan which became the cornerstone that formed the company's financial education wings.

They conduct live workshops, online programs, and one-on-one personal development and results coaching. The first edition of Financially Speaking: The Best Improvement Starts with Self-Improvement was self-published in 2008, the second edition was released in 2016.

Michael will also publish entertaining and exciting books for pleasure reading with his upcoming Romance-Mystery-Suspense Novel series. Watch out Alex Cross!!!

As an author, Michael's love and passion for writing has led him to write both fiction and non-fiction books for the sole purpose of educating and entertaining the planet! Property investing and land banking can also be added to his generational wealth building portfolio.

Not coming from generational wealth as a child; he became an avid student of the game of basketball. Starting with his high school championship winning coach; Michael was taught early on; how to win in the game of basketball as well as how to win in the game of life. He understood the value of coaching then; as he fully understands the value of coaching today.

While attending Hirsch High School, Michael was co-captain of the 1973 Boys Class AA Chicago City Basketball Champions and the Illinois High School Association (IHSA) Class AA State Basketball Championship Teams. Experiencing winning at the highest level an early age in basketball, set the tone for understanding how to win in the game of life for Michael.

The entire State Championship team was inducted into the Illinois High School Association (IHSA) Hall of Fame Class of 1993 and the Chicago Public League Basketball Coaches Association (CPLBCA) Hall of Fame Class of 2013. Michael was also inducted into Chicago Hirsch High School's Alumni Hall of Fame Class of 2016.

Michael received the 2017 – John H. Johnson, Businessman of the Year Award in Chicago. The award was presented by Creativity United "We Dream In Color" Founder; Quinton de' Alexander.

Michael did his undergraduate studies at Lincoln University in Jefferson City, Missouri, and the University of Wisconsin-Parkside in Kenosha, Wisconsin, where he played basketball at both universities.

Michael also played basketball in the European League and has traveled throughout the United States as well as to numerous countries throughout Europe. He has played with and against some of the best of the best college and professional basketball players during his era.

Michael began listening to tapes and became an avid book reader of some of the most renowned thought leaders to expedite and expand his personal growth & development. His habit and love for reading are ever present today!

While spending 30 years in the private and public transportation sectors, Michael held various management positions in the private sector. In the public sector, Michael held the operator/line instructor positions before retiring from the Chicago Transit Authority in 2012.

Michael served as the co-founder and assistant treasurer of the "Blessed to Invest" Investment Club, where his personal growth/development & financial education became an everyday habit of choice.

His call to service became real because of his burning desire, and his heartfelt mission is to give back to society. During his employment with the Chicago Transit Authority, he regularly donated to the Historically Black Colleges and Universities Scholarship Fund to help grow our future leaders.

He continues his heartfelt mission to give back by donating a portion from his book sales to causes dear to his heart to uplift the lives of men, women, and children by offering them a hand up and not a handout! With your purchase of his books, along with your continued support of Michael`s other upcoming projects, you will be giving back as well. Remember, "Teamwork, makes the Dream-work."

Michael and his wife Robbie, along with a group of like-minded, socially conscious investors, together, donated over 3 million sandwiches back to the community. Feeding America`s hungry is the service-driven mission of this special group.

He is also an advisory member of the Always Already Amazing Charitable Foundation in Chicago. Together we assist, inspire, change and transform the lives of children, seniors, and Veterans using various programs. Michael also donated his time to help raise funds for The Golden Wings Helping Hands Foundation, also located in the Chicagoland area. The funds are used to create personal hygiene care bags that are donated to the homeless.

Michael and Robbie created their online course titled; "Live W.E.A.L.T.H.Y., The 7 Principals to Guide Your Journey to Abundance." Financial freedom is just one click away. For more info, visit our website at www.tmeginc.com.

Michael and Robbie enjoy being of service to others while using personal growth and development along with continuing financial education to advance their opportunities to serve at a higher level. They enjoy traveling while

Internationally Speaking and meeting new and exciting people from other cultures, from around the world.

Go to the YouTube link and watch a short video for more information about his book titled: Financially Speaking: The Best Improvement Starts With Self Improvement https://youtu.be/rwQ99S2C5Ac.

Visit his website at www.tmeginc.com - to claim and receive your free gift "while they last."

THE MATHEWS ENTREPRENEUR GROUP INC (TMEG)
PRESENTS
It's Time to Get Serious
FINDING YOUR MOMENT OF CLARITY
DISCOVER YOUR POWER WITHIN
BY
AUTHOR
MICHAEL BART MATHEWS
INTERNATIONAL SPEAKER, FINANCIAL
TRANSFORMATION COACH
1020 PARK DRIVE, SUITE 491
FLOSSMOOR, ILLINOIS
60422-1711

MOBILE DIRECT: +1 708/997/3508
WHATSAPP +1 708 997 3508
OFFICE: +1 708/377/4688

PERSONAL EMAIL: mikemath73@gmail.com
BUSINESS EMAIL: info@tmeginc.com
WEBSITE: www.tmeginc.com

LinkedIn: https://www.linkedin.com/in/
michael-bart-mathews-ceo-4a351512/
Facebook Personal: https://www.facebook.
com/michaelbartmathews
Facebook Business: https://www.facebook.com/tmegroupinc
Instagram @ MichaelBartMathews
TWITTER: @mikemath73

To purchase a copy of Michael's books:
*Financially Speaking: The Best Improvement Starts With Self
Improvement-Create Your Own Economic Stimulus Plan*
www.tmeginc.com or www.amazon.com
Go to the YouTube link and watch a short
video for more information about Financially
Speaking https://youtu.be/rwQ99S2C5Ac

Visit his website www.tmeginc.com - to
claim your free gift "while they last."

THE
MATHEWS
ENTREPRENEUR
GROUP, INC.

Printed in the United States
By Bookmasters